MW01181964

Praise for

Making Referral Relationships Pay:

*A Complete Guide to Revenue-Sharing Partnerships
for Financial Advisers and CPAs*

by Thomas Grady

"As a CPA and a CFP practitioner, I find Thomas Grady's book to be a practical how-to guide on how financial advisers can work in a productive and profitable manner with CPAs. **I wish this book had been available when I was a CPA first trying to break into the financial-services business.**"

> JEFFREY H. RATTINER, CPA, CFP, MBA
> President and CEO, JR Financial Group
> Author, *Getting Started as a Financial Planner*

"A well-written, comprehensive guide to working with CPAs. **I would recommend this to anyone who wants to grow a practice through referrals.**"

> JOHN D. ANDERSON
> Managing Director, SEI Wealth Network

.

Making Referral Relationships Pay

Also available from Bloomberg Press

Building a High-End Financial Services Practice
by Cliff Oberlin and Jill Powers

The Financial Services Marketing Handbook
by Evelyn Ehrlich and Duke Fanelli

Practice Made Perfect
by Mark C. Tibergien and Rebecca Pomering

Virtual-Office Tools for a High-Margin Practice
by David J. Drucker and Joel P. Bruckenstein

The New Fiduciary Standard
by Tim Hatton, CFP, CIMA, AIF

Deena Katz on Practice Management
by Deena B. Katz

Deena Katz's Tools and Templates for Your Practice
by Deena B. Katz

In Search of the Perfect Model
by Mary Rowland

*Getting Started as a Financial Planner:
Revised and Updated Edition*
by Jeffrey H. Rattiner

_____

A complete list of our titles is available at
www.bloomberg.com/books

ATTENTION CORPORATIONS

THIS BOOK IS AVAILABLE for bulk purchase at special discount. Special editions or chapter reprints can also be customized to specifications. For information, please e-mail Bloomberg Press, **press@bloomberg.com**, Attention: Director of Special Markets, or phone 212-617-7966.

Making Referral Relationships Pay

A Complete Guide to Revenue-Sharing Partnerships for Financial Advisers and CPAs

Thomas Grady

BLOOMBERG PRESS

NEW YORK

First edition published 2006
1 3 5 7 9 10 8 6 4 2

Library of Congress Cataloging-in-Publication Data

Grady, Thomas
    Making referral relationships pay : a complete guide to revenue-sharing partnerships for financial advisers and CPAs / Thomas Grady.-- 1st ed.
    p. cm.
    Summary: "Explains the business-structure and regulatory steps for setting up compensation-sharing partnerships between financial advisers and CPAs. Includes perspectives of registered representatives (governed by the NASD) and the registered investment adviser (governed by state laws and by the Securities and Exchange Commission). Also addressed: hybrid case of dual registrations. Includes a regulatory overview, case studies, and sample documents"--Provided by publisher.
    Includes bibliographical references and index.
    ISBN 1-57660-182-X (alk. paper)
    1. Investment advisors--Legal status, laws, etc.--United States. 2. Accountants--Legal status, laws, etc.--United States. 3. Investment advisors--Fees--United States. 4. Accountants--Fees--United States. 5. Investment advisor-client relationships--United States. 6. Strategic alliances (Business)--Law and legislation--United States. 7. Business referrals--United States. 8. Partnership--United States. I. Title.
    KF1072.G73 2006
    346.73'0926--dc22

                                                    2005030383

To Charlotte, my far better half of thirty-eight years,
and our children, Brian, Rehanna Leigh, and Laura.
And to our lone grandchild at this moment, Garet.

Contents

Acknowledgments

Thanks to:

Jim Evens, Jim Matush, Eric Steiner and Alan Smith, Jen Yarbro, Joanie Lewis, Kathryn Moore, and Bill Bounds of Trinity Wealth Advisors for their patience and input.

David Fingerhut of Legacy Financial Group for his input on NASD compliance and compliance software.

Janet Bamford, my editor on this project, for her excellent work in checking all my details for accuracy, clarity, and sanity.

Introduction

MANY CERTIFIED PUBLIC ACCOUNTING (CPA) firms share clients with investment advisers on a reciprocal basis. The vast majority of this sharing—in either direction—is done as a professional courtesy, meaning no compensation passes between the investment adviser and the CPA firm when revenue is generated from the shared client.

As investment advisers and CPA firms know, this method of referral—void of compensation—is not always balanced. More often than not, either the investment adviser or the CPA firm sends fewer referrals through the mutual gate, causing the strategic alliance to deteriorate and finally cease. In the rare instances of success, equilibrium acts as a sort of "good faith" compensation. The referral flow remains healthy and so does the strategic alliance.

CPA firms have their own reasons that might prevent the sharing of revenue, reasons couched in professional interpretation of what is right for their clients and their practice. The investment adviser does not have the same limitations. As heavily regulated as the investment profession is, the investment adviser can share compensation with CPAs—albeit under very specific circumstances.

This book examines in practical detail how investment advisers and CPA firms can solidify their strategic alliances by allowing the CPA firms to receive a share of investment advisory compensation. Paying the CPA firm helps minimize the possibility that the stream of referrals will dry up because of imbalance. Even if the investment adviser sends no clients through the mutual gate to the CPA firm, sending money is tantamount to the same action.

The investment adviser (registered representative [RR], registered investment adviser [RIA], or both) and the CPA firm must know and understand the investment compliance and regulatory entanglements they face if the investment adviser wishes to dole out compensation to the CPA firm in exchange for referrals. In most cases, the responsibility for assuring investment compliance sits more squarely in the investment adviser's lap. But it is critical that the CPA firm understand the investment regulatory issues in order to make the best decisions about how to structure a strategic alliance with the investment adviser.

Here are a few of those issues that are examined in more detail in the chapters that follow:

Types of Compensation—There are two methods of investment compensation: commissions and fees. They are distinctly different. The first is regulated by the Securities Act of 1934 and the second by the Investment Advisers Act of 1940. Can the investment adviser offer both to the CPA firm? If so, which best fits the strategic alliance?

Business Structure—Should the CPA firm become: 1) a registered rep with the same brokerage firm as the investment adviser; 2) an investment adviser registered with the investment adviser's RIA; or 3) an owner of the RIA itself? Or should the CPA firm become merely a solicitor?

Licensing—There are various types and levels of licenses required, depending upon which type of compensation and which business structure is selected. Then again, under some specific circumstances, the CPA firm doesn't have to become licensed at all.

Client Disclosure—How much information about their strategic alliance do CPAs and investment advisers need to disclose to clients? Depending on which organizational structure is chosen, the degree of disclosure required runs the gamut from complete and straightforward to obscured by paperwork to buried deep in the adviser's Form ADV, the disclosure form filed with regulators.

Client Communications—How heavy a regulatory hand can be tolerated by the CPA firm? In some brokerage firms, weeks can pass before a simple letter to the client is approved by the compliance department. In other firms, a copy of a letter sent to a client is merely kept on file.

Income Taxes—When money changes hands, the IRS demands its share. How this investment compensation is taxed to the CPA firm is directly related to the type of compensation and the business structure chosen.

Continuing Education—In some cases, a CPA might spend six to ten hours annually taking tests. In other cases, there are no continuing-education requirements.

Expense of Operation—Complying with investment regulations isn't just a once-a-year or even once-a-quarter exercise. Compliance is so pervasive that it has worked its way deeply and expensively into the daily operations of most investment practices. Most. Not all.

Audits—Does the CPA firm want to be audited: 1) annually by a brokerage firm; 2) annually by a branch office; 3) sporadically and without announcement by the National Association of Securities Dealers (NASD), the Securities & Exchange Commission (SEC), or a state regulatory body; or 4) never? Audits can be as intrusive as a request to inspect all e-mails sent to and received from clients.

And finally, the ever-present disclaimer:

This book covers complex regulatory disciplines and various other less intricate ones. However, it cannot replace the advice of proper legal and tax counsel when parties have advanced into the realm of acute due diligence in their search for a strategic alliance. This book should be used as a detailed opening primer to the process.

Making Referral Relationships Pay

1 | Money Talks

Revenue sharing in this book refers to an arrangement whereby an investment adviser shares with a CPA firm compensation (whether from commissions or fees) that is generated from client referrals the CPA firm makes to the investment adviser.

Revenue sharing in nearly all service professions is regulated to some degree, so attempting to examine the reciprocal gesture of an investment adviser referring clients to a CPA firm is beyond the scope of this book. In other words, we're going to focus exclusively on the legal and compliance issues and the avenues investment advisers and CPA firms can take in order to legitimately share revenue on referrals delivered by the CPA firm to the investment adviser.

A referral relationship between an investment adviser and any CPA firm that does not include revenue sharing is almost certainly doomed. Here's why.

We hold these facts to be universally true and dear to our hearts (we are, after all, capitalists):
—money and time are equivalent
—money pays the bills
—money motivates
—money is quantifiable
—money is a wise collectible
—money is security

Now let's examine the antitheses to these:
—without money, your time has been wasted
—without money, creditors begin stalking you
—without money, there is no progress in building your business
—when there is no money, you can't count it to measure your success
—when there is no money you can't invest it or squirrel it away as savings
—without money, you're living in a cardboard box down by the river

Most of us would agree that not every facet of our lives revolves around money—nor should it. However, without money, or at least the minimum amount of money each of us deems essential, the other facets of our lives become minimal and stark.

So money talks—and talk alone does not.

The "All-Talk" Alliance

Just the thought of dragging your brain through the vast, complex quagmire of investment regulation to determine the dos and don'ts of a revenue-sharing alliance is enough to cause a migraine. So sharing revenue is not often done, and potential partners rely on the all-talk alliance instead. The problem is that commitment in an all-talk arrangement eventually wanes, degraded by time, inactivity, referral imbalance, a knowledge void, and competing influences.

To commit is defined by our handy Webster's as "to bind or obligate, as by pledge or assurance." If we pledge or assure something, we certainly expect some similar tangible and measurable pledge or benefit coming back to us. Without reciprocity, commerce perishes. Because money is the reciprocal unit of commerce, why not use it?

Let's take a look at two levels of commitment: one without money and the other with it.

You're a partner in a reputable CPA firm in town. A tax client with a $6 million investment portfolio tells you her stockbroker makes her very nervous, what with all the phone calls and commissions and her exasperated uncertainty about his investment recommendations, which seem endless.

"What are my alternatives?" she asks you.

"You should call Jimmy Joe Bob at JJB Investment Advisers," you tell her. "They do a very good job. They've helped a number of our firm's clients." The client writes down JJB's phone number.

Conversation over. That's it! That's the extent of the qualifying referral. But when the CPA firm receives shared investment revenue on that $6 million portfolio, the commitment runs deeper. Same client, same request for help; but your reply differs.

"Our firm has a strategic alliance with JJB Investment Advisers," you tell her. "What that means is we assist you in making decisions about your investments with JJB. We also consult with them on their investment decisions involving your specific tax issues. We attend all meetings with you and JJB. If you'd like I can set up our first meeting with Jimmy Joe Bob, president of JJB, for next week."

Be assured that the client's $6 million is as good as transferred to JJB's control and, because of the fees shared on the $6 million portfolio, the CPA firm just increased its profit margin.

Having a hidden agenda is shady business behavior, but unfortunately, it's not unusual. It's the first and, many times, the only cause of the disintegration of the all-talk relationship. A typical hidden agenda would be an attempt to increase revenue flow by a quick increase in a firm's client base without intending to do the same for the other side. A CPA or CPA firm operating in this mode encourages the investment adviser to immediately refer clients, knowing full well it will be mostly a one-way street.

If the CPA firm has this kind of hidden agenda, the all-talk relationship with the financial adviser crumbles quickly as the adviser begins to recognize that referral flow is moving in only one direction—from him to the CPA firm. If, on the other hand, a revenue-sharing alliance is established at the outset, the impetus for a hidden agenda vanishes. Why? Money.

It's crucial to have some way to measure how productive the alliance is. Simply taking a body count of how many referrals were made by each partner is an especially flawed metric. It doesn't take into account the size of a potential client's account or how serious that client is about signing on. So this particular gauge is insufficient, and depending on it can contribute to the demise of the CPA–adviser relationship. For reasons discussed in the Introduction, the number flowing in either direction is rarely equal, so it soon becomes obvious when one side performs while the other only talks.

In a revenue-sharing alliance, the money sent from the investment adviser to the CPA firm is quantifiable—and spendable. The number of referrals exchanged—equal or unequal—doesn't matter. If the CPA firm decides to stop sending prospects, the money ceases. Not a healthy business decision. Yet even if the investment adviser sends only money and no referrals in the CPA firm's direction, it's highly unlikely the CPA firm will become agitated and terminate the alliance.

An old friend and business associate once coined the phrase: "Say it and forget it; write it and regret it." His ditty refers to accountability, but the first part of the phrase captures the notion of the all-talk arrangement. It's always couched in a verbal agreement—or what is more graciously characterized as a gentlemen's agreement. Nothing goes on paper; therefore nothing in the alliance ultimately matters.

The device that ends this is the legal business model and its attendant documentation, which includes the regulatory and business structure arrangement between the investment adviser and the CPA firm—signed, launched with champagne, and abided by. The legal business model compels commitment, removes hidden agendas, and establishes a means of measurement.

A legal business model moves the relationship from all-talk to revenue sharing. The key word here is legal. A business model or document involving an investment adviser and any CPA firm that is legal must pass successfully through two decision-making processes: regulatory and organizational.

The Fundamentals of the Legal Business Model

Investment regulation affects the final decision of how to structure the business relationship more significantly than organizational factors do. So examining regulatory issues first will lend more clarity and shape to the decision about how to organize the alliance and which business entity to employ. There is a bewildering number of investment rules and regulations pertaining to and influencing various types of strategic alliances. All must be understood.

Organizational issues are less complicated and relate to what structural business entity best fits the party's tax ramifications, as well as what fits all of the preferences formed while examining regulatory matters.

The entire relevant content of each is heavily scrutinized throughout the rest of this book. Right now, let's look at a snapshot of what's ahead.

Regulatory Considerations

In any professional service, market violations over time force the profession to adopt specific behavior mandates imposed either via self-regulating organizations or by government law. The investment advisory world has not escaped either of these two watchdogs.

The Laws and Compensation

Regulation is always based on law (or in some instances a code of ethics). In the case of the investment profession, the financial shenanigans before and during the Great Depression caused investment industry behavior to be governed by two laws (and the subsequent rules and regulations that continue to be adopted as a result of evolutions in the market): the Securities Act of 1934 (hereafter referred to as the 1934 Act) and the Investment Advisers Act of 1940 (the 1940 Act). These are very different laws applying to very different types of behavior.

The 1934 Act regulates commissioned activity. The 1940 Act regulates fee-based activity. These are two very basic descriptions. Each is accurate in its fundamental qualifier. However, each unfolds in more convoluted detail, as we see in Chapter 2.

The Securities and Exchange Commission (SEC), in most cases, is the governing body that has the authority to enforce both the 1934 Act and the 1940 Act and to regulate the behavior of individuals operating under them. In addition, a self-regulating organization (SRO) called the National Association of Securities Dealers (NASD) oversees the behavior of all those individuals operating under the

1934 Act. The NASD has no jurisdiction or regulatory power over those individuals operating under the 1940 Act.

The phrase heard most often to describe a person operating under the scrutiny of the NASD is registered rep, short for registered representative (RR). With what organization is this person registered? The NASD. No one can engage in investment activity, on behalf of the public, that pays a commission, until that person becomes a member of the NASD, holds the appropriate licenses, and affiliates with a brokerage firm. This is crucial information when organizational decision time arrives.

Another phrase heard more often lately is registered investment adviser (RIA). An RIA is paid in fees. There is no self-regulatory organization that hovers over RIAs. The only governing body of an RIA is either the SEC or the state in which the RIA is domiciled.

Should a CPA firm enter a strategic alliance with an RR or an RIA, or both? Does the CPA firm want to collect commissions or fees—or both? We scrutinize this critical question more thoroughly in Chapters 6 and 7.

Ongoing Compliance Requirements

Registered representatives (1934 Act) and the brokerage firm that they are either affiliated with or employed by must navigate a labyrinth of daily compliance exercises and duties, ranging from retaining and signing trade blotters to preserving all incoming and outgoing e-mails.

In addition to the anxiety associated with whether the RR's office is properly executing all elements of daily compliance, the cost of such compliance can be monumental: specially trained staff, compliance officer, storage space, technology, sheer quantity of paperwork, and the looming threat of audits.

If a CPA firm is pondering whether to strategically align with an RR office, these factors cannot be discounted simply because the CPA firm is off-site, or not housed in the same building. In most of the cases examined in this book, the CPA firm is regarded as a satellite of the RR's office and is subject to the same compliance criteria and processes as the RR's office.

Registered investment advisers (1940 Act) have far fewer compliance regulations to cope with in their practices. On a scale of one to ten, with the burden of complying with RR regulations being a ten, RIA compliance is a two. So the time and cost burden is substantially less.

Licensing (The Authority to Do Business)
Both RRs and RIAs are required to be licensed. There are three elements to licensing: testing, errors and omissions (E&O) insurance, and continuing education. The complexity of each is a direct reflection of the laws that govern it. These factors are an expense of doing business and are time-consuming.

1934 Act—RR
♦ **Testing:** Commission is the revenue of the RR. Commission can be paid only to a human being (not a business entity) who is:
1 a member of the NASD,
2 properly licensed, and
3 affiliated with a brokerage firm.

To become a member of the NASD, an individual must pass one or more of the securities examinations the organization requires. Properly licensed means the RRs may dispense investment advice only on those types of securities they have studied and for which they have passed examinations certifying their competence. If an adviser hasn't fulfilled all of these conditions, he or she can't receive commissions.

♦ **E&O insurance:** To-date there is no NASD rule or SEC law requiring that an RR acquire and maintain E&O insurance. That's not the case with brokerage firms. Because brokerage firms are always hauled into arbitration right alongside the RR when an infraction is claimed by a client, firms consider it crucial that all parties have some professional liability insurance. So RRs employed by or affiliated with brokerage firms must obtain E&O insurance, usually through the brokerage firm. Arbitration cases have increased 60 percent since the market bubble burst in early 2000, and the cost of E&O insurance has increased proportionately.

♦ **Continuing education:** The NASD requires "no-fail" testing every two years for each license held. If an RR holds the Series 7 license, only a single test must be taken. "No-fail" means what it implies: failure is not an option. The RR, during a single testing session, continues answering questions until a certain percentage are answered correctly.

1940 Act—RIA

♦ **Testing:** RIAs receive revenue in the form of fees directly from the client. On the federal level, the authority to act as an RIA does not originate from passing a test but from the proper filing of a document called ADV. The SEC has no testing requirements. However, most states do have testing requirements.

♦ **E&O insurance:** As with RRs, there is no law that stipulates an RIA hold E&O insurance. Under some circumstances, some do. Most do not.

♦ **Continuing education:** RIAs are not obligated by any regulatory body to engage in continuing education.

Audits

Any one or all of several regulatory bodies can conduct audits. The factors exposed to an audit depend on a number of elements surrounding the investment firm or office. But the audit atmosphere and potential consequences for an RR are quite different from those for an RIA.

1934 Act—RR

Usually the word "audit" causes everybody some anxiety. But audits of RRs tend to cause even greater discomfort. Very often those being audited have only a modest grasp of the 1934 Act and the rules adopted since its passage, all of which govern their daily activity. And they're well aware of their lack of knowledge, so when auditors show up, RRs often know there are skeletons waiting to be found but don't know in which closets.

The bodies authorized to audit RRs are:

♦ the SEC (unannounced and at random)
♦ the NASD (unannounced and at random)

♦ the regulatory entity of the state of domicile (unannounced and at random)

♦ the affiliated brokerage firm (scheduled and annual)

1940 Act—RIA

Because RIA licensing (or the authority to do business) is not a product of testing but merely the result of the submission and acceptance of Form ADV, what is audited is essentially the content of the ADV and how well the RIA adheres to the document.

Before any client signatures are laid down, an RIA must provide a copy of its ADV to prospective clients. The ADV contains information about how the RIA operates as an investment adviser. It is detailed and exhaustive to the point that clients should have no questions or doubts about an RIA's methods of service and investment policies.

Auditors compare what an RIA's Form ADV states to how the RIA behaves, evidence of which is contained in files and paper flow. The RIA had better be doing what it tells the public it's doing. In essence, the RIA establishes the framework of its own audit.

The bodies authorized to audit RIAs are:

♦ the SEC (unannounced and at random)

♦ the regulatory entity of the state of domicile (unannounced and at random)

The means of authority bestowed upon the state of domicile to audit RIAs is the Series 65 test, which is discussed in greater detail in Chapter 2. The test is compulsory.

To reiterate what was stated at the outset of this brief on regulatory issues—investment behavior by financial advisers is rooted in the 1934 Act and the 1940 Act and all their subsequently adopted rules. Each law governs a clearly dissimilar type of financial adviser: the 1934 Act for RRs and the 1940 Act for RIAs. Each type of financial adviser is unmistakably different, because the methods of compensation and the types of disclosure required for such compensation are different.

The depth and breadth of the issues in the regulatory category are by far more pronounced than those of the organizational category.

Organizational Considerations

Organization includes not only the legal business model (if any) chosen to house the alliance but also the development of the process and procedures that will be followed by the CPAs and investment advisers to advance the business and generate revenue. Many such procedures of an investment business have their origins in the law. So organizational options become clearer after the parties have completed their discussions and decisions on the regulatory issues.

Fundamental policies and procedures are examined throughout the book. Summarized here are the legal business model choices, all of which are placed under a microscope in the chapters that follow.

Registered Representatives

Because RR compensation can be paid only to a human being, a strategic business alliance with an RR cannot be corporate. It is also unlawful for an RR to share commission with any entity or any other human being that is not also an RR. These facts present limited avenues:

The most basic alliance is for a member of the CPA firm to become an RR and affiliate with the brokerage firm of the initial RR in the alliance. Any adult human being with a clean moral, legal, and financial record can become a member of the NASD and therefore an RR. By doing so, the CPA firm can then share commission with the original RR at any split on which they agree.

A second alliance called "paid services," if established and managed properly, is perfectly legal. However, it can create considerable opportunity for abuse and, if captured in the net of an auditor, could trigger disciplinary action and fines.

In the paid services alliance, a CPA firm joins forces with an RR by providing the RR with a specific type of billable service in connection with clients the CPA firm refers to the RR. The amount of paid service billed is a means of "producing" revenue for the CPA firm. Notice the word chosen was "produced," not "shared"? The abuse arises when the two partners decide the amount of paid services should reflect some percent of the commission paid to the RR on referrals sent by the CPA firm.

There are two variations of the paid services alliance: rented office space alliance and consultant alliance.

The rented office space variation speaks for itself: the RR rents office space from the CPA firm, producing a revenue stream to the CPA firm, which walks potential clients down the hall for an introduction to the RR.

A second type of rented office space revenue-generator can be employed by a CPA firm with multiple partners. One of the CPA firm partners becomes an RR and aligns with an existing RR. After the existing RR removes his share of the revenue, the CPA firm and the CPA partner RR legally, although indirectly, share revenue on clients referred to the CPA partner RR by the CPA firm partners. The CPA partner RR then pays a rent to the CPA firm thereby producing revenue for the CPA firm and its other partners. This alliance places the audit onus on the CPA RR and removes it from the original existing RR. It also creates very interesting tax consequences we discuss later.

The consultant alliance is identical to the rented office space alliance except instead of buying the use of space, the RR is buying consultation. The CPA firm in the alliance invoices the RR for consultation with regard to a specific referral—who is now a mutual client. This method, too, as we shall see, can be fraught with danger.

Registered Investment Adviser

Because compensation can be more freely shared as an RIA, a multitude of business structures are available for an alliance. The structure ultimately chosen depends prominently on which of the following three means of sharing compensation are selected: solicitor, investment adviser, or owner. The single most dominant question that must be addressed is how the alliance wants to disclose the relationship to the client.

In the next chapter, we examine in more detail the rules and regulations of the two laws—the 1934 Act and 1940 Act—that are fundamental to how a strategic alliance is built. In fact, it presents a central question, one that is answered as we move through the rest of the book: how can compensation be shared?

.

2 | The Acts

Two federal laws govern financial advisers: the Securities Exchange Act of 1934 and the Investment Advisers Act of 1940. Some financial advisers—a specific class of registered investment adviser—are regulated by their domiciled state (more on this later in this chapter).

If a survey were conducted among all individuals generating a livelihood under one or both of these Acts, only a tiny fraction would know what the Acts proclaim about entering alliances and sharing compensation. Furthermore, the vast majority of this group has neither the time nor the desire to tenaciously drill into these Acts for answers. It's no wonder so many attempts at compensation-sharing relationships wilt at the dialogue stage.

As well, imagine how much more in the dark are those CPAs with whom the financial adviser wants a strategic alliance. CPAs must understand at least the legal nuances of compensation sharing if they are to execute appropriate business decisions about strategic alliances and their potential business structures.

This chapter is not intended to sink so deeply into the letter of the Acts that the reader dozes off. It focuses on which Act applies to which professional and the fundamental elements that need consideration when formulating decisions about a strategic alliance.

As the dates attached to each Act indicate, both were passed as a result of the investment misbehaviors that helped trigger the Great Depression. During the late 1920s, investment methods and procedures went largely unregulated. Greed ensured that just about every conceivable unethical act was committed on a regular basis, which caused a rapid deterioration in the integrity of the securities industry and ultimately a collapse of the market.

The banking system teetered dangerously as people stampeded to withdraw their cash. Between 1930 and 1934, more than 9,100 banks nailed their doors shut. The stock market dropped 40 percent in the three months after the October 1929 crash. One out of every four working Americans had no job. Soup kitchens opened. Lines formed. Gloom prevailed.

Capitalism was on the ropes. Congress had to act. Here's the opening statement of the Securities Exchange Act of 1934 (the 1934 Act):

> For the reasons hereinafter enumerated, transactions in securities as commonly conducted upon securities exchanges and over-the-counter markets are affected with a national public interest which makes it necessary to provide for regulation and control of such transactions and of practices and matters related thereto... *in order to protect interstate commerce, the national credit, the Federal taxing power, to protect and make more effective the national banking system and Federal Reserve System, and to insure the maintenance of fair and honest markets* in such transactions [emphasis added].

The tone of the introduction of the Investment Advisers Act of 1940 (the 1940 Act) is just as weighty:

> Upon the basis of facts disclosed by the record and report of the Securities and Exchange Commission... and facts otherwise disclosed and ascertained, it is hereby found that investment advisers are of national concern, in that... their advice, counsel, publications, writings, analyses, and reports customarily relate to the purchase and sale of securities traded on national securities exchanges... *the*

foregoing transactions occur in such volume as substantially to affect interstate commerce, national securities exchanges, and other securities markets, the national banking system and the national economy [emphasis added].

The 1934 Act, among many regulatory stipulations, created the Securities and Exchange Commission (SEC) and established its authority over all things investment. Nothing falls outside the edges of its umbrella.

Then why was the 1940 Act necessary?

Each Act pertains to a different type of investment adviser. In the simplest of terms, the 1934 Act regulates advisers receiving commission as compensation, and the 1940 Act regulates those receiving compensation directly from the client, or in other words, those receiving fees. But both Acts, and all the investment behavior regulated by them, fall within the jurisdiction of the SEC. This is important to remember because in Chapter 5 we discuss auditing authority.

The 1934 Act

About ten years after the 1934 Act passed, it became clear that monitoring the behavior of so many people and processes having to do with investment was an incredibly daunting task for the SEC, already a thriving government bureaucracy. The National Association of Securities Dealers (NASD) sprang from this burden.

Officially a self-regulating organization, the NASD can better be described as a private club. If an individual wants to receive commission from sales activity in the investment world in the United States, she must join this club, which has specific rules and regulations that must be followed. (Neither the 1934 Act nor the NASD has any jurisdiction over advisers who receive fees and not commissions.)

The reason for characterizing the NASD as a private club is that some of its rules and regulations probably abridge a few of its members' individual rights as guaranteed by the United States Constitution. But by joining the club, members agree to forgo those protections and abide by all the rules and regulations. If violations occur, membership is yanked and the member is booted out onto the sidewalk, which means commission for investment activity can no longer be received and a career in the securities business is over.

The 1934 Act provides the foundation for some of the NASD's rules and regulations. But most have been added since the NASD was formed.

Because the sharing of revenue (in this case commission) is the major factor in the success of a strategic alliance between a financial adviser and the CPA, it is essential to understand the NASD in order to make appropriate decisions about the structure of the strategic alliance.

So, stepping into the shoes of a CPA, let's join the NASD and see how it works and what it means to be an active member.

Becoming a Member of NASD

With a staff of more than 2,000 and a budget of $400 million, the NASD oversees 5,200 brokerage firms, 96,000 offices of brokerage firms, and 664,000 individual members who man those offices. Most of these individuals are registered reps. An RR receives commission for buying and selling securities on behalf of the public.

An individual cannot become an RR independently of the NASD. A person must first be affiliated with one of the 5,200 brokerage firms and then pass one or more of various securities tests crafted by the NASD.

Here's what Rule 15b7-1 says:

No registered broker or dealer shall effect any transaction in, or induce the purchase or sale of, any security unless any natural person associated with such broker or dealer who effects or is involved in effecting such transaction is registered or approved in accordance with the standards of training, experience, competence, and other qualification standards (including but not limited to submitting and maintaining all required forms, paying all required fees, and passing any required examinations) established by the rules of any national securities exchange or national securities association of which such broker or dealer is a member or under the rules of the Municipal Securities Rulemaking Board (if it is subject to the rules of that organization).

Individuals cannot take the NASD tests without being affiliated with a brokerage firm. The documentation that executes this affiliation is a Form U-4. (An RR exiting a brokerage firm completes Form U-5.) Form U-4 asks the applicant numerous questions, most of which pertain to the applicant's background: education, employment experience, legal entanglements (if any), and soundness of personal finances (for example, has the applicant ever declared bankruptcy). Falsifying an answer on the U-4 makes the applicant a criminal, which will prevent that person from becoming an RR and might put the applicant in a prison cell somewhere.

Even though someone is affiliated with a brokerage firm, that person is forbidden to give advice to the public on securities until he has successfully passed the specific test that gives him the authority to give advice on those specific types of securities. If that person does hand out his opinion without first passing the appropriate test, he'll never get a chance to take that test; his new brokerage firm will promptly *dis*affiliate with him, because *it* will be in violation of the rules and regulations as a result of his actions.

There are two types of RR affiliations: employed and independent. An employed RR is one who actually works for a brokerage firm (Merrill Lynch, AG Edwards, etc.) and can be fired. The independent RR is in business for himself and, in effect, hires a brokerage firm (Royal Alliance, Raymond James, etc.) to accommodate NASD activity and custodial demands for clients. (These differences are examined more minutely in later chapters.)

There are three tests most commonly taken to become an RR:

Series 6 authorizes the sale of open-end mutual funds, variable life insurance, and variable annuities. It is a moderately difficult test of 100 questions for which the CPA is given two hours and fifteen minutes to answer; currently it costs $60 to take the test.

Series 7 authorizes the sale of everything in Series 6 plus individual stocks, bonds, options, closed-end mutual funds, and direct participation programs (such as limited partnerships). This test has been described by many who have taken it as one of the most grueling marathons they've ever endured. It is a six-hour mental migraine requiring 250 answers. And for this, the CPA pays $200.

Series 63 is required by the CPA's state of domicile in order to render advice within its borders; some states may require additional testing. The Series 63 is the tamest of these three tests. The CPA is allowed 75 minutes to answer 65 questions at a cost of $70.

In summary, if a CPA is considering becoming a member of the NASD as an avenue to his strategic alliance with a financial adviser, who is already a member of the NASD, he'll need one of these two combinations:

◆ Series 6 *plus* Series 63 *plus* any additional testing required by the CPA's state
◆ Series 7 *plus* Series 63 *plus* any additional testing required by the CPA's state

Once the CPA passes a given NASD test, the CPA is a member in good standing of that organization and can deliver advice on the authorized security types and, what's just as important for our purposes, receive commission as the result of action taken on the CPA's advice by a client. Commission arrives in many forms, from many sources, but it is all funneled through the brokerage firm. (A key nuance: this means no individual can accept payment from a client for writing a financial plan; an RR cannot charge for such service because it is regarded as a fee and not commission.)

An important consideration in deciding what structure a strategic alliance should take is the fact that neither the 1934 Act nor the NASD requires RRs to make an unequivocally clear and perpetual disclosure of commission—how much and whence it comes. Clients rarely know how much commission is generated from individual products sold to them, who receives it, and how long that commission stream persists. They can find out by either asking the RR or (sometimes) sinking deeply into the product prospectus and hoping for three things: 1) to locate the information, 2) to comprehend the intricate legalese in which it is presented, and 3) to avoid contracting a headache from the tiny four-point type. A client is unlikely to undertake any of these exercises.

However, disclosure of two other matters is a key element of membership in the NASD and is important to decisions about the nature of alliances: product offerings (or prospectuses) and broker-age firm affiliation. The NASD's rationale is that the client must be aware of as many characteristics of her engagement as possible, from the broadest (brokerage firm affiliation) to the most minute (details in the prospectus). Because the RR is registered with the NASD, the client can assume (not always justifiably) that the RR is pristine. As a practical matter, it is the client's responsibility to make certain of this. Anyone can do so by contacting the NASD for information on a specific registered rep.

Product Offering Disclosure (The Prospectus)

With the exception of individual equities bought on the secondary market, there are prospectuses for all security products offered by RRs. Inside these, in excruciating detail, is a thorough revelation of the product itself. Most prospectuses are mammoth in volume and exceptionally difficult to understand, and are therefore rarely opened by the client.

Some commonly known shortcomings of prospectuses are mentioned here because they give rise to some important realities:

1 An RR typically gives advice and hopes the client accepts it by purchasing an offered product that fulfills the advice; the RR's compensation does not come from the advice but from the purchased product.

2 Reading the product's prospectus breeds confusion and questions.

3 Confusion and questions can be impediments to the sale of the product.

4 Therefore, many RRs regard the prospectus itself as a threat to their commission.

5 To those RRs, the awareness that the client seldom reads these documents is an unspoken comfort.

Brokerage Affiliation Disclosure

The moment clients step into an RR's presence, they must be informed with which brokerage firm the RR has an affiliation. If the RR's affiliation is via employment, then such communication has already taken place because the brokerage firm has its moniker splashed across office walls, stationary, and business cards. Disclosure case closed. For the independent RR who hires a brokerage firm as a vendor for custodial purposes, the obligation to immediately disclose may require more effort. Most independent RRs harbor a deep-seated posture of, well, independence. They bristle at being perceived as associated with anything institutional. In these cases, clients will likely find brokerage firm affiliation disclosures on small subtle plaques hung quietly on office foyer walls, and the RR may need to make explicit mention of the relationship.

In summary, if the CPA and RR choose commission as a means of shared compensation (perhaps because it's hidden from the client), the CPA will need to:

♦ affiliate with the RR alliance partner's (not just any) brokerage firm
♦ join the NASD
♦ pay for and pass at least two tests, one of which is potentially grueling
♦ abide by the terms of the 1934 Act and the NASD rules and regulations

These tasks allow the CPA to join in a strategic alliance as an RR with an existing RR. The "to-do" list grows longer, though, as the business activity of the alliance accelerates. The additional items are burdens of operation that are covered in later chapters.

The 1940 Act

The 1940 Investment Advisers Act primarily regulates two somewhat similar entities: investment companies and investment advisers. For the most part, "investment companies" is a fancy phrase for mutual funds. Both entities covered by the 1940 Act do fundamentally the same thing: advise on and execute the purchase of securities for investors who have empowered them to do so on their behalf. The topic of investment companies is well beyond the purpose of this book, so let's get right to the topic of investment advisers.

The 1940 Act uses the term "investment adviser," but a registered investment adviser (RIA) is the title of choice among advisers. An RIA is registered with the SEC, a requirement before the adviser can market his or her skills to the public.

(An important note: Using the acronym RIA as though it signified a professional designation such as CFP or CPA is illegal; in communicating with the public, "registered investment adviser" must be spelled out in its entirety. This book is not intended as communication with the public and therefore, for the purpose of simplicity, the acronym is employed.)

Unlike the RR, the RIA has no self-regulating organization like the NASD. Though the issue has been discussed over the years, in May of 2000, an SEC-sponsored roundtable of eight securities experts concluded that an SRO for RIAs was not only unnecessary but unwanted.

Words from that roundtable reflect concurring sentiments:

> We are concerned, there has been this steady drum beat and talk about regulatory black holes and the fact that there seem to be these problems. I simply don't see them...There are no documented cases of persistent frauds and abuses like you have on the broker/dealer side...So I hope maybe today we can all agree that an SRO is absolutely unwarranted.
>
> —Bradley W. Skolnik, President, North American Securities
> Administrators Association, Indiana Securities Commissioner

> We have concluded that no SRO is needed...an SRO is unnecessary and inappropriate for the investment advisory and financial planning community...there's no evidence of a serious flaw in the present and state structure and it seems to be regulated well.
>
> —Phyllis Bernstein, Director of Personal Financial Planning,
> American Institute of Certified Public Accountants

I concur that we probably don't need an SRO for investment advisers. I think the [1940 Investment Advisers] Act works well, as I said earlier.

—Roy T. Diliberto, President, The Financial Planning Association

There are two firmly connected reasons why the 1940 Act alone is sufficient regulation for investment advisers, rendering unnecessary the massive assistance of a self-regulating organization like the NASD: 1) the lack of a trading/settlement/custodial infrastructure and 2) the method of RIA compensation.

As mentioned earlier, the NASD's rules and regulations apply not only to the conduct of RRs but to the processes, procedures, and behavior of its 5,200 member brokerage firms and their interrelationships. Because an RR's commission on securities activity executed on behalf of a client is controlled by and must come from or through the affiliated brokerage firm, the RR is inescapably attached to the whole apparatus.

An RIA has no need of a brokerage firm to collect compensation. RIA compensation is fee-based, including payment for written financial plans. Fees are retrieved directly from the client, not from the hidden conduits of an affiliated brokerage firm. This fact will perhaps be the most vital element of alliance decision-making and business structure.

Individuals or entities "register" with the appropriate governing body to become RIAs. There are two potential governing bodies: the SEC and the RIA's state of domicile. Up until the mid-1990s the SEC was the sole governing body for all RIAs. But because the adviser population quadrupled from 6,000 in 1988 to 23,000 in 1996, the SEC, as in the mid-1940s with the 1934 Act, was again overwhelmed as a watchdog. Legislation was passed that flung off from the SEC's shoulders all but roughly 7,000 investment advisers. Where did their regulatory oversight go? To the individual states in which the investment advisers were domiciled. What criteria were used to determine which RIAs remained under the jurisdiction of the SEC? Assets under management. The parameters were simple:

If an RIA managed:

♦ less than $25 million, it belonged with the state of domicile
♦ more than $30 million, it belonged with the SEC
♦ between $25 million and $30 million, the RIA made the choice

These levels are in effect today. When each state was made responsible for regulatory governance of low-dollar RIAs within its boundaries, state legislators had a decision to make: does the state write its own securities laws to govern its new RIAs or does it simply adopt the terms of the 1940 Act and all subsequent rules? This author did not canvas the states to determine their decision. However, grapevine has it that most, if not all, chose the easy path and adopted the 1940 Act terms.

There are no testing requirements to register as an investment adviser with the SEC. Most states, however, do call for some testing. The most common requirement is the Series 63, defined earlier.

Unlike the RR who generates compensation on the sale of products to fulfill advice given, the RIA produces compensation on advice given. The RIA's compensation comes directly from the client. Simply put, the client of an RR marries the product; the client of an RIA marries the RIA.

The purpose of a prospectus is to inform the client of the RR's product offering. The RIA must have a similar document that informs the client of the RIA's process, procedures, and investment policies. That document is called an ADV.

In addition to educating the client, the ADV also provides the means of registering the RIA with the appropriate governing body. The ADV has two parts. Both parts must be filed upon registration. All registrations, even state-domiciled registrations, originate through the SEC's Web presence, the Investment Adviser Registration Depository (IARD). For an RIA with too few assets under management, the SEC merely funnels the ADV to the appropriate state.

ADV Part I provides information to the RIA's regulatory body. It does not have to be made available to the client. Part I presents details about RIA ownership (direct and indirect), percentage ownership, and the persons or entities (if any) that in turn own and control the RIA owners. It also elicits extensive information about the financial and legal integrity of each owner. When significant changes occur within the RIA, such as a change in ownership, those changes must be submitted to the regulators.

ADV Part II provides information to the client. It is also submitted to the governing body through the SEC. Part II presents the following details about the business practices, investment methods, and procedures of the RIA: services and fees, types of clients, types of investments employed, methods of analysis and sources of information for making decisions, education and business standards of its advisers, "other business" activity, conditions for managing accounts, investment brokerage discretion, and a balance sheet. Part II must be handed to the client prior to the signing of any contract.

Revenue-Sharing Methods

Unlike the 1934 Act and NASD, the 1940 Act permits direct revenue sharing. Because of this, strategically aligning with an RIA offers greater flexibility. There are three methods of sharing RIA fees with other entities or individuals: 1) become a solicitor for an RIA, 2) register as an individual investment adviser of an RIA, and 3) take an ownership position in an RIA. Each of these is couched firmly in the 1940 Act. For the purposes of this chapter, the three methods are discussed only briefly. In Chapter 7, each is thoroughly dissected and placed under a strategic alliance microscope.

An ownership position is disclosed in ADV Part I, investment adviser status in ADV Part II, and identity as a solicitor in a direct, signed client disclosure. The degree of disclosure required is just as significant to a decision on how to strategically align with an RIA as the perceived degree of commitment to referrals.

Degree of Disclosure

♦ *Ownership position*—ADV Part I is not given to the client, so ownership position remains private
♦ *Adviser status*—ADV Part II (on average, a twenty-page document) is given to the client
♦ *Solicitor identity*—Clients referred to an RIA by a solicitor must sign and receive a copy of a Solicitor's Disclosure Agreement,

which details the fee-sharing arrangement between the RIA and the solicitor

In summary, if fee-based advice fits a CPA firm's concept of a strategic alliance, then that firm and its potential investment partner must decide which of the three methods of sharing revenue best suits their relationship. Each requires specific and different preparation procedures and documentation.

A Note on "Duals"

From a legal perspective, a dual is a business entity that is simultaneously registered as a brokerage firm and an RIA. For example, Merrill Lynch is a brokerage firm and an RIA; it's called a dual. For our alliance purposes, however, a dual is a human being. It is an RR who is also an investment adviser of an existing RIA. Duals take on various configurations, each of which has a different impact on the potential characteristics of a strategic alliance:

♦ An RR is an employee of a brokerage firm; the brokerage firm is an RIA; the RR chooses to be an investment adviser for the brokerage firm RIA.
♦ An RR is an independent registered rep who affiliates with a brokerage firm; the brokerage firm is an RIA; the RR chooses to be an investment adviser for the brokerage firm RIA.
♦ An RR is an independent who affiliates with a brokerage firm; the RR is an independent RIA, which is completely unassociated with the brokerage firm.

A number of factors contribute to how those characteristics differ under each of these circumstances. As well, in the first arrangement, there can be variations from brokerage firm to brokerage firm on issues of strategic alliances involving their RR/investment advisers.

In Summary

The two Acts passed by Congress long ago regulate every aspect of the domestic investment world. But the single most important set of regulations that will provide a footing for how a strategic alliance takes shape concerns compensation.

If an investment adviser and a CPA are considering an alliance, a few questions may already be under consideration:

♦ Do they share commission, fees, or both?
♦ How private do the alliance members want the nature of the compensation to be?
♦ What licenses does the CPA want to attain?
♦ How simple or complex does the alliance have to be?

The compensation setup will always be chosen from the same menu, either:

♦ registered rep (commission),
♦ registered investment adviser (fees), or
♦ dual (both).

The strategic alliance members must choose one of these. What is appropriate for them will become clearer as we move through this book.

The next chapter delves into how regulations affect organization (and vice versa) of RRs and RIAs, including a more intricate review of compensation and how it is received, various revenue-sharing models, and assorted potential alliance business structures.

3 | Regulations and Registered Representatives

The facts we know about registered representatives (RRs) are:
—They are regulated by the Securities Act of 1934
  —They receive commission as compensation and they cannot accept money directly from a client
  —Their primary means of disclosure is a product prospectus
  —They can be a dual registrant, that is, an RR and an investment adviser on an existing RIA

We also know that RRs must always be affiliated with a brokerage firm and that they come in two varieties: employee and independent. Because each of these two varieties of RRs has different corporate/ business influences and obligations, each brings different options to the alliance table. In this chapter, these differences are discussed.

Actually, the nature of the RR's brokerage firm itself is the key to knowing into which category the RR falls. There are two types of brokerage firms: employer and independent. An employer brokerage hires RRs as employees. (Some examples of employer brokerage firms are AG Edwards, Merrill Lynch, and Wachovia.) Independent brokerage firms market themselves to independent RRs, who are self-employed. (Examples of independent brokerage firms are Linsco Private Ledger, Royal Alliance, and Raymond James.) Both types of brokerage firms have ultimate responsibility for all compliance and regulatory matters concerning their RRs. This is tantamount to control and, as might be expected, is a sensitive area for the independent RR.

Employed Registered Reps versus Independent Registered Reps

From a business perspective, these two types of RRs operate in dramatically different ways. From a compliance perspective, they are identical.

Sharable Commission

An employed RR (ERR) has little or no business overhead: no cost for rent, marketing materials, utilities, stationary, business cards, office equipment, general personnel, daily operations, and finally, no indirect cost of compliance. The independent RR (IRR) bears the burden of all these costs.

Obviously, there has to be a corresponding imbalance on the compensation side. There is. An ERR forfeits to the brokerage firm far more commission on the sale of products than does the independent. The ERR's brokerage firm on average slices off 60 percent of the commission and passes the remainder on to the ERR. The IRR's brokerage firm on average keeps 10 percent and pays out 90 percent.

From the CPA's perspective, the ERR brings far fewer compensation dollars to the alliance than the IRR. On a $2,000 compensation sale the ERR brings $800 to the table. The IRR, on the same sale, offers up $1,800. If the alliance calls for a fifty-fifty split, which one is more appealing?

Some products offer the hope of greater compensation for the ERR. We analyze those and other specific products in this chapter under "What Products Generally Pay."

Corporate Sway

The IRR's brokerage firm has the same compliance control and responsibility over the IRR as the ERR's brokerage firm has over the ERR. But that's where the power similarity ends. The IRR is literally in business for himself and maintains complete autonomy from the brokerage firm on all matters not associated with compliance and regulation. As an employee of a brokerage firm, the ERR can be fired. The IRR's brokerage firm, by contrast, is a vendor to the IRR's business and it can be fired by the IRR. There are roughly fifty independent brokerage firms clamoring for the attention of over 75,000 IRRs.

So the IRR maintains greater control over business operations, including flexibility and decision making with regard to strategic alliances. For example, a CPA might decide to establish a strategic alliance with an existing IRR, move into the same office space with the IRR, and share clients and compensation in both directions. This arrangement would never be allowed in the office building of most employee brokerage firms. In short, the ERR must acquire approval from brokerage firm authorities for any strategic alliance, whereas the IRR is the authority.

In addition, image might be a cause of concern for the CPA of a strategic alliance. If the CPA values autonomy from the corporate world, an association with an ERR and the brokerage firm may not be suitable.

Logistics

Most employee brokerage firms house their ERRs in central locations (one building or a campus) in one or more cities throughout the country. All the ERRs are required to herd together under one roof primarily for operational efficiency, economics, and management of compliance (it's easier and less costly to keep an eye on them when they're all in one place). Rarely, if ever, does an employee brokerage firm allow an ERR to operate alone from home or a leased office. This means the CPA in a strategic alliance with an ERR would have to maintain an office at the brokerage firm's location, which probably would not be terribly conducive to the routine of the CPA's core business.

By contrast, the business model of independent brokerage firms, by necessity, is built around "branch" and "satellite" offices. Most independent brokerage firms have a single location they call national headquarters, and all the IRRs the firm serves are scattered across the country in branch and satellite offices (including many in individual homes) that are not owned by the brokerage firm.

A branch office of an independent brokerage firm is a location from which one or more of its IRRs conduct business. A satellite office is a branch of a branch office. So, for compliance responsibility purposes (which we delve into in Chapter 5), the hierarchy looks like this:

♦ **First level:** National Headquarters
♦ **Second level:** Branch Office
♦ **Third level:** Satellite Office

If a CPA does not want to share office space with an IRR when they engage in a strategic alliance, the existing business office of the CPA becomes a satellite office of the IRR's branch office.

♦ **First level:** National Headquarters
♦ **Second level:** IRR is the branch office
♦ **Third level:** CPA's existing office is the satellite office

There are two types of satellite offices: registered and unregistered. An unregistered satellite is one in which all identification, including mailing address and phone number, must point to the satellite's branch office. If the CPA's office at 123 Main Street is an unregistered satellite of an RR branch office at 123 Washington Street, then the CPA office must indicate on all client communications that its office is located at 123 Washington Street. A registered CPA branch office can claim and broadcast its own communications and location identification. The trade-off is that the registered satellite office will be audited annually by the branch office compliance officer.

Prior to the development of the Internet, securities activity between IRRs in branch and satellite offices and their national headquarters where trades are executed was performed by telephone. The presence and speed of the Internet has handed IRRs the capacity to place orders from their offices. This has lowered the cost of trading dramatically by eliminating the phone calls and reducing the number of headquarters order-takers. It has also made opening and maintaining branch and satellite offices far easier.

The Registered Rep and Commission

Commission flows in a number of directions through multiple securities industry players before it's tucked away into the RR's pocket. The complexity of this traffic is enhanced by the movement of RRs throughout their careers from brokerage firm to brokerage firm. The method used to ensure the precision and accuracy of all this activity is a coding system.

The Channels

When individuals join the NASD, they do so through the NASD's Central Registration Depository (CRD) system. The CRD is a computerized database containing security information about RRs, brokerage firms, and investment advisers. The system provides the RR with a unique number. That number remains the property of the RR throughout his or her career in the industry. Even if the RR becomes an RIA and stops being an RR, as the RIA, he or she still retains that original number.

This is only the start of codes. When an RR affiliates with a brokerage firm, that firm assigns the RR a unique code, referred to as a rep ID (for example: U787). This rep ID is the property of this specific RR within the brokerage firm. Both independent and employer brokerage firms practice this rep ID assignment system.

Exclusive codes are also given by independent brokerage firm headquarters to each branch and each satellite they serve. Most employer brokerage firms do the same for each of their locations throughout the country. This system allows the routing of commission through these codes rather than through the names of firms or individuals.

If a CPA establishes a strategic alliance with an existing RR (IRR

ERR: an employed registered rep working directly for a brokerage firm. IRR: an independent registered rep who is self-employed and contracts with a brokerage firm to handle issues of compliance, custodial, and trading.

or ERR), in order to share commission on referred cases, the CPA must become an RR. The CPA affiliates with the existing RR's brokerage firm and is provided a unique rep ID. Each RR in the strategic alliance has a different rep ID.

In order to share commissions on alliances, most brokerage firms treat both RRs as one and assign the tandem RR unit a unique rep ID of its own. The two RRs instruct their brokerage firm on the agreed-upon percentage split of their strategic alliance (say fifty-fifty), the brokerage firm pays 100 percent of the commission to the single unique tandem rep ID, which then splits the payment into 50 percent to one RR ID and 50 percent to the other RR ID. So the ultimate commission payment ends with a human being…and can go no further.

Brokerage firms (both independent and employer) maintain selling agreements with investment product manufacturers, largely mutual fund families and life insurance companies, which sell annuities. Full commission from the sale of these products must go directly to the brokerage firm, which then passes it down through its coding and rep ID maze to the RR.

What Products Generally Pay

To accomplish a client's investment objectives, an RR has a multitude of products from which to choose. The compensation thrown off by each is different in amount and in frequency.

Mutual Funds

Mutual funds are the most actively sold investment product. Mutual fund families usually manufacture three variations of each fund, defined by share class: A shares, B shares, and C shares. Each has a singular load structure and therefore a singular commission amount and payout schedule.

HERE'S THE COMPLETE channel of commission from ABC mutual fund family's growth fund Class A share sale to a strategic alliance of an RR and a CPA (who is also an RR):*

♦ ABC mutual fund family, CRD number 5987412-6, sends $10,000 commission check to

♦ Brokerage firm, CRD number 7856992-4, which removes its 10 percent and sends $9,000 to

♦ Branch office, brokerage code TR543, which passes it through to

♦ Satellite office, brokerage code TRA543, which passes it through to

♦ Strategic alliance, rep ID B678, which splits it into two, at $4,500 each, and sends one check to

♦ Original RR, rep ID B254, and the other to

♦ CPA RR, rep ID B987.

* Throughout the book, CRD and rep identification numbers are fictitious examples and any correspondence to actual numbers is coincidental.

Class A Shares

The client forfeits a specific percentage—from 2 percent to 6 percent (average of 5 percent)—of the amount committed before the fund shares are purchased. Most of this is commission and starts its trip through the commission channel. Upon the first-year anniversary of the client purchase and every quarter thereafter, a gross fee equal to 0.0625 percent (in most cases) of the fund balance enters the commission channel. This commission is called a 12b-1 fee and it pays for the fund family's marketing expenses—in other words "commission." Note that the SEC limits 12b-1 fees to 1 percent of assets annually, of which a maximum of 0.25 percent a year may go to a registered representative.

For example:

—A client writes a check for $20,000 to be invested in one of ABC's mutual funds,

—The IRR makes the purchase via the Internet and sends the check to his brokerage firm,

—The brokerage firm sends $20,000 to ABC funds as payment for the shares,

—ABC Fund Company sends a $1,000 load (5 percent of $20,000) back to the brokerage firm,

—The brokerage firm removes its 10 percent ($100) and sends the balance down the commission channel.

Commission on Class A shares has an automatic suppressant in breakpoints, a series of rising dollar levels at which clients receive discounted loads. The levels vary among mutual fund families, but below is a typical structure:

Level	Rate	Example		Commission*
$0 to $99,999	5.0%	commission on $99,999	=	$ 4,999
$100,000 to $249,999	4.0%	commission on $200,000	=	$ 8,000
$250,000 to $499,999	3.0%	commission on $400,000	=	$12,000
$500,000 to $999,999	2.0%	commission on $800,000	=	$16,000
$1,000,000 to $4,999,999	1.0%	commission on $1,600,000	=	$16,000
$5,000,000 and over	0.0%			

*These figures are gross commission. Net to the RR will be less, depending upon what percentage is removed by the brokerage firm before being sent down the commission channel.

This breakpoint concept is often overlooked, not only by novice RRs (until their brokerage firm reminds them before a sale takes place), but more importantly by CPAs who are analyzing the revenue impact of a strategic alliance they are considering. Forgetting these schedules during this due diligence can be devastating. If, after reviewing a client base, a CPA decides in favor of a strategic alliance while overlooking breakpoints, there is trouble ahead. Shock will quickly set in when the CPA begins studying for the NASD tests and realizes that gross commission on the $800,000 sale above is $16,000, not $40,000.

Class B Shares

The client forfeits nothing upon purchase. However, attached to this class of shares is a contingent deferred sales charge (CDSC), commonly referred to as a backload. The contingency is the length of time the investor agrees to own the shares. On average the client must own Class B shares for six years before the CDSC is removed and the shares convert to Class A. If the client sells the positions before the sixth year, the sales charge is removed from the proceeds before being sent to the client. Normally, the deferred sales charge commences at 6 percent and drops 1 percent per year of share ownership. The CDSC essentially traps the client long enough so the fund family can recoup the commission it paid to the RR.

Even though a commission has not been immediately deducted from the client's account, the RR still receives an immediate commission, which is, on average, slightly less than that of the Class A shares. The mutual fund family itself is the source of the commission. If the client exits the fund positions he trips the CDSC wire, which the mutual fund family uses to recover a portion (probably calculated after hours of study by actuaries) of the gross commission it fronted the RR. The portion not recovered from the departing client has been siphoned off each fund at an average of 1 percent per year as a 12b-1 fee during the years invested. So the net expense ratio of an average Class A growth fund of 1.28 percent becomes 2.28 percent on Class B shares. When the CDSC perishes after the sixth year, Class B shares slip into Class A status and 0.75 percent of the expense fee vanishes. The other 0.25 percent remains as the standard 12b-1 fee discussed earlier: annually, paid quarterly to the RR as gross commission.

Class C Shares

Once again, the client forfeits nothing upon purchase. With Class C shares also comes a CDSC. In most cases, however, its life span is a single year. And its deferred rate is only 1 percent. The RR immediately receives 1 percent (gross) of the invested amount, paid by the mutual fund family. Then every quarter after the first year, the RR receives one-quarter of 0.75 percent (gross) of the balance in the funds as a 12b-1 fee. Combine this with the standard 0.25 percent

12b-1 fee these shares also deliver, and the RR receives 1 percent per year (gross) of the asset balance in these funds.

This becomes a quasi, "buried," assets under management fee, which, in some cases, the clients discover only if they stumble across it in the prospectus. Ethical RRs will divulge to the client all this additional fee baggage prior to the purchase of Class C shares. But it's almost certain the topic will stay unmentioned after the initial revelation, and because the extra 1 percent cannot be found on monthly statements, the whole commission matter falls into the out-of-sight, out-of-mind category.

Class C shares are the most expensive class of shares to own long term, which means for many clients they are inappropriate. So the NASD frowns deeply on RRs employing them exclusively (or even primarily) to create a steady stream of future income, or what the NASD refers to as "annuitizing your business." In fact, if surveillance departments at most brokerage firms detect a single RR selling Class C shares too often, the RR will be contacted for written justification.

Class C shares are falling out of favor with clients, with regulators, and with the industry. Recently, one major mutual fund family discontinued selling Class C shares, and other firms are expected to follow.

The Variables: Annuities and Life Insurance
The word "variable" in front of the terms "annuity" or "life insurance" means the product is a security and therefore is regulated by the 1934 Act and the NASD. Fixed annuities, whole life insurance, and term life insurance are not securities and can be sold by individuals not belonging to the NASD.

Residing inside variable annuities and variable life insurance are sub-accounts, which are almost identical to mutual funds, which is why they're considered securities. Details of the differences go beyond the scope of this book, but they generally pertain to expense structure. What is distinctly different is the method and amount of commission generated from variable annuities and variable life insurance. On neither product is commission related to any element of the sub-accounts contained within.

Variable Annuities

The client forfeits nothing upon the purchase of a variable annuity. But almost all annuities carry a CDSC. If the client bails out of the annuity before the final year of the CDSC, that client is penalized at the rate assigned to the year of exit. The rates and duration of the CDSC are related to the amount of commission thrown off by the annuity.

In most cases, there's a direct positive correlation between the duration of the CDSC and the amount of commission. When one goes up so does the other, and the longer the duration of the CDSC period, the more commission the RR takes home. Average duration is seven years, and, as with mutual funds, the rate charged to the client upon early exit generally slides downward by 1 percent per year.

Average industry commission on a seven-year CDSC annuity is 5 percent. And because clients pay nothing from the outset, there are no breakpoints and thus no sliding deterioration of commission. If the $800,000 mutual fund investment mentioned earlier were an annuity, it would indeed spin off the full $40,000 gross commission, the RR receiving his or her net portion after the brokerage firm's cut.

There are assorted structures for delivering annuity commissions. These structures are designed and controlled by the insurance company that manufactures the annuity, not by the RR's brokerage firm. These structures range from delivering the commission in a one-time lump sum, as in the $40,000 example above, all the way to distributing a 1 percent lump sum and then, after the first year, 1 percent per year forever, or as long as the client holds the annuity contract and as long as the RR remains an RR.

Here's an example of a simple delivery structure for gross annuity commissions:

♦ 5% up front; 0.00% per year on asset balance in sub-accounts
♦ 4% up front; 0.25% per year on asset balance in sub-accounts
♦ 3% up front; 0.50% per year on asset balance in sub-accounts
♦ 2% up front; 0.75% per year on asset balance in sub-accounts
♦ 1% up front; 1.00% per year on asset balance in sub-accounts

Some insurance companies have designed their annuity contracts so that the lower the up-front amount an RR accepts, the lower the

CDSC duration the client must bear. The NASD's warning against "annuitizing your business" with Class C share mutual funds does not apply to annuities. Some insurance companies charge back an RR a portion of the initially paid commission if the client leaves the contract early. The amount is prorated for the lost time in the contract.

Variable Life Insurance

A universal calculation for variable life insurance commissions does not exist. Generally, the starting point for determining commissions is the "target premium," an amount that is rarely equal to the premium the client actually pays. The variable element of variable life insurance means the client can pay a premium amount somewhere in between a minimum (the amount that must be paid to keep the policy in force) and a maximum, relative to the death benefit, that the IRS will allow to be paid. Some policies allow consumers to set their target premium once—and then they have to stick to it—but some allow policyholders to vary payments from month to month. Establishing a target premium somewhere in the middle is necessary to create a fixed point from which commissions can be calculated. Ascertaining the target premium of a variable life insurance policy is an internal function of the life insurance company. The RR receives some given percentage of the initial target premium, normally ranging from 100 percent to 60 percent.

Because both target premium and percentage payout can fluctuate from one insurance company to another, both factors must be considered when determining commissions paid. One policy might have a 90 percent payout on an annual target premium of $12,000, producing a $10,800 commission. An identical insurance policy with another company might pay 75 percent on an annual target premium of $14,000, throwing off $10,500 of commissions.

Stocks and Bonds

The amount of commission paid to RRs on the buying and selling of individual securities, like stocks and bonds, varies so widely among brokerage firms that attempting to pin down an average is futile. One caveat, though: most independent brokerage firms serving IRRs usually install a commission payout on this trading activity that is markedly lower than their payout for the other three product lines (mutual funds, variable annuities, and variable life insurance). For example, one of the largest independent brokerages pays only 70 percent to its IRRs on securities trading, yet pays out 90 percent commission on the sale of all else. Unlike the other three products, securities trading is manned within the walls of the brokerage firm and is therefore a direct and hard cost to the firm. Thus the lower payout.

Authority to Advise

Remember these two testing requirement combinations outlined in Chapter 2?

◆ Series 6 *plus* Series 63 *plus* any additional testing required by the state.
◆ Series 7 *plus* Series 63 *plus* any additional testing required by the state.

If the first option is chosen, which authorizes mutual fund advice only, and a client places a brokerage statement in front of the RR that contains five mutual funds and five individual stocks, the RR cannot utter a single word about the stocks. Some regulators would take the position that the RR cannot even give advice on the mutual funds because they are part of an entire portfolio that includes stocks, on which the RR is not licensed to advise, and the portfolio in its entirety is a reflection of the client's investment and risk profile. Thus, giving advice on the mutual funds is the same as giving advice on changing the risk composition of the profile, which might then change the status of the stock positions. All this is synonymous with giving advice on the stocks. According to this interpretation, the RR has violated NASD rules simply by discussing the mutual funds.

Potential Alliances

Sharing commission with a nonregistered person: this is against the rules.

Sharing commission with a business entity: this is also against the rules.

Operational (business) alliances with an RR: these are not against the rules, but caution must be taken when structuring these alliances to ensure there is no hint of direct commission sharing relative to commission generated from referrals provided the RR by the CPA.

Leasing and Operational Costs

Most solo-practitioner CPAs or CPA partnerships have office space they maintain where they conduct business. The CPAs either lease space or own the building in which they reside. If they lease space, there is usually a clause that allows them to sublease any additional space they do not occupy.

If a CPA has such space, it can be leased monthly to an RR. Provisions of the lease might also include variable costs for copying, faxing, phones, conference rooms, common areas, bathrooms, and so forth. This arrangement provides financial motivation for the CPA to refer clients to the RR. It is certainly a weaker incentive than direct, relative compensation, but extra revenue nonetheless. If the CPA stops walking referrals down the hall or the referrals don't materialize, the RR gives notice that the monthly lease has ended, and the revenue flowing to the CPA from the lease and all the ancillary services evaporates.

The leased office may or may not be the RR's sole office, but it must be a branch office or a satellite of a branch office. If the RR is affiliated with an employer brokerage firm, it can't establish the office in the CPA firm as a branch without the permission of the firm (and it is unlikely the brokerage firm would approve the arrangement). An IRR has complete freedom to establish this office-leasing alliance. If it is the RR's only office, the chances of the alliance succeeding increase dramatically, eliminating the effects of the old adage out of sight, out of mind.

It is essential that lease revenue flowing back to the CPA be detached from the amount of commission the RR receives for referrals from the CPA. The strategic alliance can accomplish this by fixing the monthly rent rate. This fixed rate and its duration must resemble other rental arrangements prevalent in the local market.

Variable costs outlined above, however, are another matter. As the term implies, the more activity generated from all sources, including referrals by the CPAs, the greater the need for the ancillary services and therefore the more they will cost per month. Despite the flexibility with these costs, relativity must prevail; these costs cannot take on the appearance of commission sharing.

Consulting Services

This strategic alliance is similar in concept to the leasing and operational cost alliance. But instead of leased space and office operations, the CPA provides consulting services to the RR on professionally germane topics associated with referrals the CPA sends to the RR. The CPA then invoices the RR for time and materials.

The amounts of a series of invoices cannot reflect a consistent percent of the commission thrown off by the referral cases the invoices represent. The amounts must be discernibly random.

CPA—NASD Bound

The CPA affiliates with the existing RR's brokerage firm, passes appropriate tests, and becomes a member of the NASD. This is the purest strategic alliance between an RR and a CPA—although certainly not the simplest for the CPA, as witnessed by the testing requirements. When the CPA becomes an RR and joins the existing RR in an alliance, clients are made aware of this joint work on their behalf. All applications and related documentation are signed by both parties of the strategic alliance, as required by the NASD. There is no relational veil or ambiguous revenue-sharing agreements. The strategic alliance holds itself out to the public, specifically the CPA's clients and prospects, as a team with a regulatory stamp of approval, monitored by the compliance arm of the alliance brokerage firm. Office proximity of each alliance member relative to the other is inconsequential, although one must be a satellite of the other or they must both be satellites of an existing branch office.

CPA Conduit to Partners

In a multipartner CPA office, a single partner or manager can enter into a strategic alliance with an existing RR by becoming an RR. Together they can share commission. The CPA/RR then allocates a certain amount of office space and time to being an RR, which translates into expenses to the CPA's firm. The firm then invoices the CPA for these expenses.

This method allows, and encourages, the CPA's partners to refer their clients to the strategic alliance, thereby invoking elements of both the leasing and operational cost and the consulting services arrangements. But the flow of money back to the CPA's firm must withstand the same relative-to-commissions tests of each arrangement.

There are income tax implications with this method. The CPA who is also the RR will incur all the tax ramifications of this alliance. Care must be taken not to reflect any adjustments made in the expense amount back to the CPA's firm.

In Summary

Facts about registered reps:
—They are regulated by the 1934 Act
—They receive commission as compensation and cannot accept money directly from a client
—Their primary means of disclosure is a product prospectus
—They can be a dual, or an RR and an investment adviser on an existing RIA
—There are two types of RR: employed RR (ERR) and independent RR (IRR)

Employed RR versus Independent RR

From the CPA's perspective, a strategic alliance with an IRR versus with an ERR means:
—Higher potential revenue
—More freedom and flexibility in how the alliance is structured
—Preserving independence from the corporate world
—Ease and cost of establishment

Dissecting Commission

Facts about commission:
—Commissions cannot be shared with a person who is not an NASD member, nor can they be shared with a nonperson
—A code system is employed by the NASD to track the flow of commission
—Class A share mutual fund loads are commissions and are paid directly by the client
—Commissions on all other mutual fund classes are paid by the mutual fund, which recovers it gradually from the client with higher internal 12b-1 fees and CDSCs
—Consistent use of Class C shares by an RR will draw close attention from the brokerage firm's compliance officers, concerned with "annuitizing" business revenue.
—The amount of annuity and life insurance commission is unassociated with the sub-accounts within the contract, but is directly related to how long a client must remain in the contract before absorbing a penalty to exit
—At independent brokerage firms, net commission on stocks and bond trading is normally lower than that of mutual funds and life insurance products

Potential Alliances

Regardless of what form a strategic alliance assumes, commission cannot be shared with persons not registered with the NASD and affiliated with a brokerage firm, and commissions cannot be shared or received by a business entity. This does not preclude options for the following types of alliances, or some blend of them:

—RR leases space and business operations capabilities from a CPA in exchange for a steady stream of referrals; lease and other payments cannot demonstrate positive correlation to commission received on referrals, collectively or individually

—CPA offers billable consultative services to the RR on referred cases; same cautionary note as the preceding item

—CPA becomes an RR and teams with an existing RR in order to share commissions on referrals, creating the cleanest of alliances

—CPA, partner of a firm, becomes an RR and teams with an existing RR to offer services to referred clients by all members of the CPA firm; expenses paid to the CPA's firm cannot be related to commission received on referral work; individual CPA/RR sustains the tax burden of all commission received

In the next chapter, the identical issues as they pertain to RIAs are examined.

4 | Regulations and Registered Investment Advisers

The facts we know about Registered Investment Advisers (RIAs) are:
- —They are regulated by the Investment Advisers Act of 1940
- —They receive fees directly from a client
- —Their primary means of disclosure is Form ADV Part II
- —They can be a dual registrant, that is, an RR and an RIA simultaneously

We also know that RIAs managing over $30 million register with the SEC, those below $25 million register with their state of domicile, and those between register with whichever of the two they choose. There is no difference in how RIAs operate under these two governing bodies. The RIA is free to bring precisely the same fee structure, policies, and procedures to the alliance table in either scenario, although this would be highly coincidental. The governing body has no influence on the strategic alliance, except perhaps on the public image that is projected based on how much in assets the RIA manages.

RIAs: Brokerage-Based and Autonomous

RIAs come in two varieties: brokerage-based and autonomous. Brokerage-based RIAs are those established and controlled by brokerage firms with which both independent registered reps (IRRs) and employed registered reps (ERRs) must affiliate. These are normally large national or regional brokerage firms, like the Merrill Lynches of the world. They become RIAs so their RRs can offer fee-based service to clients. The autonomous RIAs are all others; these advisory firms might be controlled by a single individual or business entity or a group of individuals or business entities.

The autonomous RIA is further divided into two categories: associated and unassociated. An autonomous associated RIA is owned and controlled by an independent registered rep (IRR), working quietly out of a leased office on Main Street. There are a great many IRRs who have established their own autonomous associated RIAs.

As a requirement of the Securities Act of 1934, IRRs must affiliate with an independent brokerage firm, which is probably also a brokerage-based RIA. As mentioned above, the independent brokerage firm establishes itself as an RIA so those IRRs it serves who are not autonomous RIAs (like the one on Main Street) can offer fee-based work to the clients through the brokerage-based RIA. RRs employed by a brokerage firm (ERRs) are forbidden by that firm from establishing their own autonomous RIAs. They must use the firm's brokerage-based RIA to offer fee-based work to clients.

An autonomous unassociated RIA is quite simple: Its owners, or the people who control it, are not members of the NASD. They are not RRs. They are not governed by the 1934 Act but by the 1940 Act. They cannot sell commissioned products. They have no affiliation with a "retail" brokerage firm. Small advisory firms that charge a flat or hourly fee for their financial and investment advice would fall into this category.

A "retail" brokerage firm is a type with which RRs must affiliate. An "institutional" brokerage firm is employed by an autonomous RIA to execute trades the RIA makes on behalf of clients and to act as custodian for its clients' securities. (Examples of institutional brokerages are Ameritrade Adviser, TD Waterhouse, and Schwab Institutional.)

Recall that the affiliated brokerage firm of an RR has complete responsibility for the RR's compliance. An institutional brokerage firm has no such responsibility for the RIAs it serves. The RIA itself holds that sole duty. An RIA structured as a business entity does not dispense investment advice. Investment advisers (IA) registered with the state or the SEC as members of these types of RIAs dispense such advice to the RIAs' clients and prospects. An RIA is an entity. An IA is a person. If an RIA has only one employee, then that employee is the owner of the RIA and is its sole IA. An RIA can have many owners and thousands of IAs, which is the case with the large, national brokerage-based RIAs mentioned above, where their RRs become IAs on the brokerage firm's RIA.

A lot of acronyms; here's a review:
RIA—registered investment adviser,
RR—registered rep,
IA—investment adviser.

Responsibility for complying with the 1940 Act and the RIA's own ADV is held by the RIA's owners or the people who control it. The ADV Part II is an RIA's prospectus. It is a detailed explanation of the RIA's policies and procedures, the services it offers, and the fees it charges. A routine SEC audit will likely discover whether an RIA or any of its IAs behave outside the realm of what is specified within the ADV Part II. As well, a disgruntled client finding such deviant behavior might pull the RIA into arbitration.

Control over the ADV Part II of the three types of RIAs (brokerage-based IRRs and ERRs, autonomous associated RIAs, and autonomous unassociated RIAs) is quite different and is important in understanding their flexibility and applicability to a strategic alliance. There are hundreds of employer and independent brokerage firms, and each has its own philosophies behind its ADV content and its own guidelines for revising it. An RR/IA who is considering a strategic alliance with a CPA firm should have full knowledge of the facts in its own RIA ADV Part II. These facts will provide precise information on what sort of strategic alliances can be built. If certain types cannot be developed, modifying the ADV Part II so that they can becomes a crucial first step in the alliance. The RR/IA must take this step. If those at the RIA who control the content of the ADV Part II decline the suggested changes, the strategic alliance has ended before it has ever begun.

Generally, here's a flexibility snapshot of the four types of ADV Part II:

Brokerage-based (Employer)—The ADV Part II of an employer brokerage firm is the least accommodating of the four. It is compiled for a captive, employed group of RR/IAs who have agreed to abide by the employer's policies and terms of employment. Changes to its ADV Part II would result only from significant RR rumblings within the brokerage firm, or a strategic corporate shift that would have to come from the top executives.

Brokerage-based (Independent)—A brokerage firm serving independent RR/IAs won't necessarily be more open to altering its ADV Part II as a result of input from the independents it serves. Changing the content of an ADV Part II that provides legal guidance to thousands of IAs in hundreds of markets is challenging. But because of this diversity, the ADV Part II, depending upon the assertiveness and foresight of the brokerage firm, might already contain the means to enter into nearly all strategic alliances.

Autonomous associated—These RIAs are owned and controlled by the independent RRs, and the content of the ADV Part II is the responsibility of the owner. Changes are easy and instantaneous. However, some independent brokerage firms require the autonomous associated RIA to submit its ADV Part II to their compliance department, which retains the right to edit the content. If the means of forming a strategic alliance are struck from the autonomous associated RIA ADV Part II by the compliance department, the independent RR might want to consider firing the brokerage firm and finding one that allows the wording to remain in the ADV Part II, or finding one that does not require ADV Part II submission.

Autonomous unassociated—These RIAs are owned and controlled by people or entities not affiliated with any brokerage firm. Changes made to the ADV Part II can be edited at will by the owners.

A Summary of RIA Configurations

Brokerage-based: owned and controlled by national or regional independent or employer brokerage firm, established to allow the RRs of the brokerage firm to enroll as IAs so they can offer fee-based advice to clients. For this privilege, the RR gives up a percent of the fees collected, normally the same percent the brokerage expects from commission work.

Autonomous associated: owned and controlled by an independent RR or group of independent RRs so they can offer fee-based advice to clients without using their affiliated brokerage firm's RIA. This does not preclude the brokerage firm from demanding a percent of the fee work performed under this RIA, which is wholly autonomous and unassociated with the brokerage firm.

Autonomous unassociated: owned and controlled by a person or group of people who are not members of the NASD.

Each type of RIA will bestow different degrees of flexibility on its IAs in forming strategic alliances with CPAs. In addition, participation by IAs in molding the content of the ADV Part II also varies significantly. The IAs of brokerage-based RIAs will have little or no input. The IAs of autonomous types will have a better chance for contribution and alteration.

Dissecting RIA Services and Fees

Because there are no legal or regulatory stipulations on what services an RIA can offer and because the fee a client pays an RIA comes directly from the client's pocket, a broad variety of types and scales of services exist.

Fee-Only

In fee-only arrangements, the adviser is paid solely by the client for the professional services rendered, and not as a result of the purchase or sale of any financial products. The work can be literally anything financially related, including an ongoing task such as managing a portfolio of assets. Fee arrangements can take a variety of forms, including a flat fee, an hourly fee, a percentage fee based on assets under management (or sometimes based on earned income), a performance-based fee (based on the gain in invested assets during a given period), or a contingent fee.

Advisers might charge the same client differently for different types of services. An RIA compiling a financial plan might charge a flat fee for the project, and then an annual percentage fee based on assets under management for continuing to manage a portfolio. Sometimes an adviser arranges an outsourced service such as bill paying, supervises the provider, and adds a fee on top of the provider's fee for his time and trouble.

Fee-Based

Fee-based advisers charge clients fees for their services, but they may also receive commissions from the client's purchase or sale of financial products, including 12b-1 fees, trailing commissions, surrender charges, and back-end fees. Some advisers have fee-offset arrangements for clients in which their compensation initially comes from fees, but the fees are later reduced by the commissions the adviser receives from the sale of a product.

Other types of compensation a fee-based adviser might receive could include referral fees that the adviser receives for referring the client to another product or service, or indirect compensation, like sales prizes or rewards, for recommending a product or service to a client.

Whether an adviser follows a fee-based or fee-only model, the common denominator is that the client pays fees directly. Although it sometimes happens that a client receives an invoice and writes out a check to pay a fee, it is far more common to have fees automatically deducted from a client's account.

Assets Under Management Policies and Fees

There are varying styles of managing a client's assets. The simplest and least active is to buy positions in a client's portfolio, hold and monitor them, changing very infrequently. Nothing else. This is the slimmed-down version of asset management services.

An RIA at the opposite end of the spectrum would:

—write a comprehensive or modular financial plan

—actively buy and sell at least a portion (tactical) of a client port-folio

—monitor all positions daily

—create and personally present quarterly performance reviews

—present economic/market analysis

—create annual capital gains/losses reports

—create any other report the client requests

—communicate directly with the client's CPA (alliance member) for tax purposes

—coordinate with the client's estate attorney when necessary

—provide specialized, topical, quantitative analysis upon the client's request

The RIA's ADV Part II and the fee should reflect the extent of services provided. The ADV is a legal document and must be factually accurate. The fee is a market matter and is subject to due diligence by the client. If an RIA's fees are too high relative to the degree of service, the market will inevitably perform its capitalist duty and the RIA will adjust or be eliminated from the market.

Investment Management Programs

An investment program is an RIA's method and philosophy of managing client assets. Investment policies can take many different forms employing up to six layers of professionally directed services: the RIA itself, the institutional brokerage, a platform service, third-party managers, institutional managers, and mutual funds. Two of these layers will always be present in an investment policy: the RIA itself and the institutional brokerage. The remaining four may or may not be employed.

Investment Program Layers

The RIA: the client's focal management and decision-making body

An institutional brokerage: trade execution, custodian, fee collector

A platform: Companies that maintain contractual agreements with numerous third-party managers in order to make them available to the clients of RIAs. For this service, platforms charge the RIA's clients a fee, deducted from the client's account. Platform examples include AssetMark, ADVISORport; in addition, some institutional brokerages offer in-house platforms.

Third-party managers: Discretionary asset managers unavailable from the sidewalk, accessible only through platform companies. Examples include Goldman Sachs, R. Meeder, and Litman Gregory. There are hundreds more. One of the tasks of a platform service as outlined above is to endlessly screen these countless third-party managers for the best performers and then place them on their "platform" so RIAs can access them on behalf of their clients.

Institutional managers: companies that offer third-party management directly to RIAs, without the assistance of a platform company. Examples are SEI and Lockwood.

Mutual funds: identified as a layer because, if used, there is an expense ratio, which is a fee to the client; if individual equities are directly employed in a client's account, the mutual fund fee does not exist.

Investment Management Program Fees

RIA: generally ranges from 0.20 percent to 3.00 percent per account per year

Brokerage: trading costs range from $10 to $35 per trade

Brokerage: custodial costs range from $0 to $35 per year per account

Platform: contractual service costs range from 0.10 percent to 0.50 percent per account per year

Third-party managers: fees range from 0.30 percent to 0.60 percent per year per account

Institutional managers: fees range from 0.30 percent to 0.60 percent per year per account

Mutual funds: if funds are used, expense ratios range from 0.30 percent to 2.00 percent

Management Variations

There are a few key components useful in categorizing variations in asset management programs. The variations revolve around where investment decisions originate (Internal/External) and what level of investment is pursued (Specific/General).

♦ **Internal:** investment position choices are made within the RIA
♦ **External:** investment position choices are made outside the RIA
♦ **Specific:** investment position choices consist of individual equities and/or mutual funds
♦ **General:** investment position choices consist of institutional managers

Internal/Specific

The RIA manages client portfolios consisting of individual stocks, bonds, and/or mutual funds by buying and selling these equities based on its own internal criteria and decision-making apparatus.

　　Layers Needed:

♦ RIA, fees average 1.50 percent
♦ Institutional brokerage, trading costs average $18 per trade and $20 per year custodial fee
♦ If individual equities are used, there are no additional costs
♦ If mutual funds are used, expense ratios average 1.48 percent per year

Internal/General

The RIA manages client portfolios consisting of third-party managers by hiring and firing these managers based on its own internal criteria and decision-making apparatus.

　　Layers Needed:

♦ RIA, fees average 1.25 percent
♦ Institutional brokerage, trading costs average $18 per trade and $20 per year custodial fee
♦ Platform, fees average 0.15 percent per year (this layer is an option for the RIA)
♦ Third-party managers, fees average 0.45 percent per year
♦ If mutual funds are used, expense ratios average 1.48 percent per year

External/Specific

The RIA relinquishes management of client portfolios to institutional managers who buy and sell individual stocks, bonds, and/or mutual funds within the portfolio.

Layers Needed:

♦ RIA, fees average 1.25 percent
♦ Institutional managers, fees average 0.50 percent per year
♦ If mutual funds are used, expense ratios average 1.48 percent per year

The Variables: Annuities and Life Insurance

Financial circumstances of RIA clients are no different than those of RR clients. RIA clients have as much need for variable annuities and variable life insurance as do RR clients. These products are commission-generating however, manufactured by entities outside the control of the RIA. Asset management, of course, is a service designed and delivered from within the RIA for a fee. As well, if an RIA is not also a dual (also an RR), it cannot receive the commission produced by these standard products. All of these factors put variable annuities and variable life insurance at odds with the core strategy of the RIA.

This conflict has created opportunity, and a few life insurance companies have seized this profit opening by manufacturing variable annuities and life insurance that throw off zero commission. One might automatically conclude that if there is no commission then the contracts must cost less to manufacture and that more money would stay in the client's account. One would be right. Commission and noncommission annuities and life insurance are indistinguishable with the exception of cost to the client, which is directly affected by what's left on the table when the agent isn't paid a commission.

In addition to the internal cost savings of fee-based annuities, the client has no exposure to a contingent deferred sales charge (CDSC.) After all, the annuity company does not have to recover commission; there is none. So the client can walk away from the annuity at any time, without paying any surrender fees and with no consequences (other than perhaps tax).

The "freedom to walk" concept is much the same in variable life insurance. The surrender penalty of traditional variable life insurance does not exist in no-commission insurance, where the cash value and surrender value are the same from the outset. If a client had to surrender a traditional life insurance policy, say, in the fourth year, she'd receive roughly a third of her initial investment. In the no-commission contract, all would be returned. Here's a comparison example: a commissionable (traditional) and a low-load life insurance policy of a $250,000 death benefit on a forty-year-old male, preferred (no-smoker, excellent health), with an annual premium of $1,266.10, growing at 9 percent per year:

	Surrender Values	
	Low-load	Traditional
Year five	$ 5,182	$ 1,804
Year ten	$11,526	$ 7,928
Year twenty	$32,335	$27,842

The nearly $4,500 difference in the surrender value in year twenty is essentially attributable to commissions and administration fees, neither of which are present in a low-load life insurance policy.

Fees—Who Charges Whom for What

The flow of commission paid to RRs is rather easy to track. Three entities are involved: the RR, the RR's brokerage firm, and the mutual fund family or life insurance company. Tracking the fees of RIAs can be either easier or far more daunting, depending on which among three management variations are employed by the RIA.

Internal/Specific

Decisions are made within the RIA, and individual equities are bought and sold in clients' accounts. Potential fee methods:

RIA—usually does not invoice client directly

Institutional brokerage—RIA contractually arranges with the client to have fees removed quarterly from the client's account and delivered to the RIA's master account with the same brokerage

Internal/General

Decisions are made within the RIA, and third-party managers are hired and fired on behalf of clients. Potential fee methods:

RIA—usually does not invoice client directly

Institutional brokerage—RIA contractually arranges with the client to have fees removed quarterly from the client's account by the platform service for the RIA, the third-party manager, and the platform itself. The platform service then forwards the fees to the RIA and the manager.

External/Specific

Decisions are made outside the RIA by institutional managers who buy and sell individual equities in clients' accounts. Potential fee methods:

RIA—does not invoice client directly

Institutional managers—RIA contractually arranges with the client to have fees removed quarterly from the client's institutional manager account by the institutional manager for the RIA and the institutional manager itself. If the institutional manager employs mutual funds, normally it does not assess a direct fee on the account but relies on the expense ratio of the fund as a source for its fee.

Any entities that exercise a fee debit function over an RIA's client account must have a signed agreement from the client to extract the money. Some RIAs include a clause in their Investment Policy Agreement that covers all billing periods, usually quarterly. Others ask the client to sign one for each quarter.

Variable Annuities and Life Insurance

The sub-accounts of the variable products are manageable asset positions; remember for billing purposes they're identical to retail mutual funds. RIAs can charge a fee for managing these sub-accounts, inside both annuities and life insurance contracts.

There are two ways to accomplish this: through the client's institutional brokerage account or directly from the client. It is easier and far less painful to have the fees deducted from the brokerage account than to have the client break out his checkbook every quarter. If fees are to be debited directly from the client's brokerage account, the annuity sub-accounts must reside with the brokerage firm. Therein lies the problem. Only a few institutional brokerages today play custodian to annuities, and even far fewer to life insurance contracts. If an RIA's brokerage firm cannot or will not house annuities or life insurance contracts and their sub-accounts, then the client's checkbook is the only option.

An alternate, and perhaps more convenient, fee method is to charge the client an hourly fee for the task of establishing the variable contracts and advising on a portfolio of sub-accounts, and then charge a single annual fee for review.

Built-in Vessels for Alliances

There are three general methods of crafting strategic alliances already built into the framework of the 1940 Act and subsequent SEC rulings over the years: solicitor's agreement, investment adviser, and passive ownership. There's also a fourth method—an outright merger or acquisition. There are numerous areas of concern inherent in the three built-in means, and the solutions will vary considerably. Not all of the concerns are present in all three techniques.

Here's what to be aware of:

♦ **Revenue-sharing rate:** What percentage of the assets under management fees is paid to the CPA for referred clients?

♦ **Ownership of revenue stream:** Does the CPA own the revenue that is generated from the referrals sent to the RIA?

♦ **Ownership of "booked" referrals:** Does the CPA own the rights to the clients?

♦ **Noncompete agreement:** Does the CPA sign a noncompete clause? If not, can the CPA register as an RIA, terminate the alliance, and walk out the door with the clients?

♦ **Capital contribution:** Under what circumstances does the CPA make a capital contribution to an existing RIA?

♦ **Shares owned:** Does the CPA receive stock in the RIA, and if so, what class of shares?

♦ **Net ownership:** What is the sum of the capital contribution and the value of the revenue stream? The SEC looks to this figure to determine whether or not an owner qualifies as a passive (non-controlling) owner.

♦ **Access to financial reporting:** Under what circumstances is the CPA offered the RIA's profit and loss statement and balance sheet to determine health?

♦ **Employee status:** When does the CPA actually become an employee of the RIA?

♦ **Voting rights:** Can the CPA vote on RIA issues?

♦ **Legality documentation:** When are legal documents drawn up to ensure clarity in the strategic alliance?

♦ **Tax reporting:** How is the CPA's shared revenue reported by the RIA?

♦ **Termination provisions:** How and when can the strategic alliance be terminated?

♦ **Retirement clauses (trigger and payout period):** Instead of terminating the strategic alliance, are there means for the CPA to cease sending referrals, yet continue to receive fees, and if so, for how long?

♦ **Approval method:** What methods are used internally by the RIA to approve strategic alliances?

♦ **Buyout provision:** How and when can the CPA be bought out of the alliance?

♦ **Estate provision:** Under what circumstances is the CPA's estate paid in the event of death?

♦ **Regulatory requirements:** And finally, what must be done legally to comply with each of the three methods?

With most of these questions, the two parties have great latitude. Suggestions made in the following models are those that have worked, most of the time. But the final decisions must be mutual.

Solicitor's Agreement

With this method, the strategic alliance is legitimized by a solicitor's agreement between the RIA and the CPA. The CPA can be a human being or a business entity of any kind in any profession. The solicitor's agreement legally appoints the CPA as an unregistered associate of the RIA. There are several restrictions and conditions the SEC places on the activities of the CPA that has been appointed as an unregistered associate: registration, disclosure, integrity, due diligence.

Registration

"Unregistered" means the CPA has not tested, is not licensed, and must not deliver investment advice to clients or potential clients. The CPA can, however, distribute literature about the RIA and assist in completing paperwork, as well as attend all meetings.

Disclosure

The client must have been given a Solicitor's Disclosure Statement as per Rule 206(4)-3(b). This statement must contain six pieces of information:

♦ Solicitor's name
♦ RIA's name
♦ The nature of the relationship, including a description of any other affiliation between the solicitor and the RIA
♦ An explanation that the solicitor will, in fact, be paid by the RIA for referring the client
♦ The terms of that payment, including how much and how often
♦ A disclosure as to whether the client is bearing the cost of the referral payment. In other words, are the fees being charged to the solicited client higher than the fees charged to nonsolicited clients? If they are higher, the disclosure statement must demonstrate by how much.

Also included in the statement is a clause that acknowledges the client's receipt of the RIA's ADV Part II.

Integrity

The CPA cannot be of dubious integrity, elements of which are described in subparagraphs (A) through (D), inclusive, of Rule 206(4)-3(a)(1)(ii), which states:

> The solicitor is not a person (A) subject to a Commission order issued under section 203(f) of the Act, or (B) convicted within the previous ten years of any felony or misdemeanor involving conduct described in section 203(e)(2)(A) through (D) of the Act, or (C) who has been found by the Commission to have engaged, or has been convicted of engaging, in any of the conduct specified in paragraphs (1), (5) or (6) of section 203(e) of the Act, or (D) is subject to an order, judgment or decree described in section 203(e)(4) of the Act.

Section 203(f) of the Act says the solicitor cannot already have been barred or suspended by the SEC from associating with an investment adviser or anyone else in the securities business.

Section 203(e)(2)(A) through (D) says the solicitor cannot have been convicted within ten years of any felony or misdemeanor:

A involving the purchase or sale of a security, making false statements or reports, bribery, perjury, burglary, etc. You get the idea.

B resulting from the conduct of business as a securities broker or dealer.

C involving the larceny, theft, extortion, forgery, etc. of funds or securities.

D involving the violation of various sections of the United States Code, which is where all U.S. laws are recorded and updated.

Section 203(e) of the Act says the solicitor cannot be found by the SEC to have engaged, or have been convicted of engaging, in any of the conduct specified in Section 203(e), Paragraphs (1), (5), or (6):

Paragraph (1) making a false or misleading statement, verbally or as part of any securities registration application

Paragraph (5) willfully violating a provision of the 1933 Act, 1934 Act, 1940 Act, Commodity Exchange Act, or any rules and regulations since established

Paragraph (6) willfully aiding, abetting, counseling, etc. any other person or entity in the violation of the provisions of those Acts stated in Paragraph 5 above.

Section 203(e)(4) advises that the solicitor cannot be the subject of an order, judgment, or decree that, by order of court, permanently or temporarily bans the solicitor from the securities business.

Due Diligence

There's significant legal footwork to be performed in an alliance. Ultimately who's responsible? Both parties: the CPA for providing full disclosure about the background of any and all members of its business who will be acting as solicitors, and the RIA for performing background checks of those people to the best of its ability. It is recommended the RIA use the Form U-4, described in Chapter 2. Have each member of the CPA's firm complete one. They are not submitted to any regulatory body; they are merely signed documents that describe historical behavior. The questions on Form U-4 cover all the conditions outlined above, and if the questions are falsely answered, the respondent can be held liable, and the RIA has gone a long way in protecting itself.

Points of Concern

Revenue-Sharing Rate

This can be a single percentage applicable to all fees from assets under management of those referrals sent by the CPA. Or it can be scaled upward in order to muster incentive. A starting point might be the rate institutional brokerage firm and industry bellwether Schwab Institutional requests from the RIAs it serves for sending retail referrals in their direction: 15 percent.

Ownership of Revenue Stream

Because there is no business entity co-owned by the parties of the strategic alliance, there is no means by which the CPA can claim ownership of the portion of the revenue stream generated by the clients referred to the RIA. As well, ownership implies dispensing advice, a definite no-no.

Ownership of "Booked" Referrals

An unregistered entity cannot claim ownership of any portion of assets being managed by a registered entity.

Noncompete Agreement

A noncompete agreement should be pursued by the RIA to prevent a CPA from becoming an RIA and moving clients.

Capital Contribution

This implies ownership, and a solicitor is not an owner.

Shares Owned

This implies ownership, and a solicitor is not an owner.

Net Ownership

Not applicable.

Access to Financial Reporting

If the CPA/solicitor is concerned that the RIA is not financially healthy, it might request an examination of the RIA's profit and loss statement and balance sheet.

Employee Status

The solicitor is not an employee, but an independent contractor. In fact, a clause should be included in the solicitor's agreement that makes such status very clear.

Voting Rights

This also implies ownership and does not apply.

Legality Documentation

The solicitor's agreement acts as legal documentation of the alliance.

Tax Reporting

As an independent contractor, the solicitor receives a Form 1099 from the RIA.

Termination Provisions

A means for ending the alliance either immediately or on short notice is essential for regulatory and other reasons. If the solicitor violates the law—say, by giving investment advice—the RIA must have the option of ending the agreement without hesitation. If the solicitor "goes silent" for a long period of time—perhaps twelve months—it's reasonable to question the effectiveness of the alliance. Conditions should be placed in the agreement that address a lack of referrals for a specific time frame. As part of these stipulations, the RIA might want to assign a qualifier to the term "referral," such as the amount of manageable assets.

Retirement Clauses

Not applicable here.

Approval Method

Who approves the alliance? If each party is a one-man show, a single handshake and a couple of signatures finalize the agreement. If there are partners on either side, debate and the need for persuasion can be expected.

Buyout Provision

The CPA/solicitor does not own the asset stream, so there is nothing to buy out.

Estate Provision

This also implies ownership and is not applicable to a solicitor's agreement.

Regulatory Requirements

These fall into two categories: internal and external:

Internal—The RIA's ADV Part II must indicate that it has solicitor arrangements with various sources. There is a question specifically asking if such arrangements exist (13B). If they do, the SEC wants text similar to this to be placed on Schedule F:

RIA engages professional entities via a Solicitor's Agreement to refer clients to RIA. Terms of the Solicitor's Agreement provide the professional entities with compensation for the referrals. RIA's referral agreement is in compliance with the federal regulations as set out in 17 CFR Section 275-206(4)-3, and in each state where state law requires. Each client is given a copy of the referral agreement prior to or at the time of entering into any advisory contract.

If the RIA is either autonomous associated or autonomous unassociated it controls the content of its ADV Part II and complying with these requirements is simple. If an RR is operating as an Investment Adviser (IA) under the ADV of a brokerage-based RIA (employer or independent), and that RIA does not provide for solicitor's agreements, the RR's first step is to seek a change. If the RIA declines, the IA cannot enter into a solicitor's agreement with anyone.

External—Prior to signing the RIA's Investment Policy Agreement, the client is provided 1) the RIA's ADV Part II, and 2) the Solicitor's Disclosure Statement. The client signs the statement and receives a copy. The RIA retains the original in the client's file.

Investment Adviser

An investment adviser (IA) comes in two forms: on-site and off-site. The on-site IA maintains an office at the RIA's place of business, is actively engaged in the pursuit of clients, and regards the position as full time. The off-site IA has no permanent presence within the RIA's offices, pursues clients only incidentally, and works part time. The off-site IA might be a retired on-site IA who still wants to dabble. The RIA regards the on-site IA as a controllable person, much like an employee, and considers the off-site retiree as a lingering on-site IA.

A CPA who becomes an off-site IA is a good potential partner for an RIA in a strategic alliance. There are two major differences between a CPA firm becoming a solicitor and a CPA firm becoming an off-site IA: licensing and degree of disclosure. Referring clients as an off-site IA requires less obtrusive disclosure but requires testing.

Let's look at all the points of concern for deciding if the IA structure is appropriate for the alliance.

Points of Concern
Revenue-Sharing Rate
An off-site IA will expend roughly the same energy as a solicitor in searching out potential referrals, which is the basis for employing the same rate: 15 percent. (An on-site IA will command a much higher rate—as high as 25 percent.)

Ownership of Revenue Stream
As with the solicitor, there is no business-entity basis for the IA (even an on-site IA) to make claim to owning the revenue stream of those clients referred.

Ownership of "Booked" Referrals
Ditto.

Noncompete Agreement
Because the CPA is a properly licensed IA, a noncompete agreement becomes even more imperative. The CPA might well decide at a later date that the clients he pushed through the RIA's door would be a nice client base with which to start an RIA and reap the full 100 percent of fees charged.

Capital Contribution
Because the off-site IA is not an owner in the RIA, this is not an issue.

Shares Owned
Ditto.

Net Ownership
Not applicable.

Access to Financial Reporting
As with the solicitor, the RIA must decide whether it wants to share its financial data with the IA.

Employee Status
The CPA is employed elsewhere and acts as an independent contractor.

Voting Rights
No ownership; no voting rights.

Legality Documentation
There are no documents required to legalize this alliance. The two parties, however, might have some peculiarities they want formalized.

Tax Reporting
Independent contractors receive 1099s.

Termination Provisions
As a licensed IA, the CPA knows the law and should be fully aware of all the elements of the RIA's ADV Part II. Violation of any provisions of either of these would justify ending the alliance. In addition, as with the solicitor, the off-site IA might have period-certain quotas it must adhere to or the alliance comes under review for effectiveness.

Retirement Clauses
If a CPA firm IA slips into overall retirement phase, the amount of referral activity might be found anywhere on a spectrum. The number of referrals might dry to zero—at which time termination occurs—because the IA intends to truly retire and engage in nothing but lazy rounds of golf. At the other end, the IA, realizing the simplicity of the arrangement, might increase activity by engaging in golf... but with potential referrals only.

Approval Method
The method is the same as with the solicitor model.

Buyout Provision
The IA owns neither the revenue nor the assets that produce the revenue, so there can be no buyout.

Estate Provision
Same as solicitor.

Regulatory Requirements
Brokerage-based RIAs will require that the CPA become an RR affiliated with its firm before allowing it to take on the role as an IA with the RIA. If an independent brokerage firm requires its approval of certain provisions of autonomous associated RIAs owned by its RRs, the RR must inquire about the proper order in which things must proceed. Does the CPA firm first have to become an RR with the independent firm before becoming an IA on the RR's autonomous associated RIA? If the independent brokerage firm chooses not to maintain edit power of its RR's RIA ADVs, then the RR is free to add a CPA firm to its RIA as an IA. Autonomous unassociated RIAs have the sole authority to add and subtract IAs.

The IA is listed in the RIA's ADV Part II, which also provides such data about the IA as education history, employment history, licenses held, and the like. One factor exclusive to this choice relative to the other two is that the CPA, depending on what profession practiced, might be required to put disclosures of his or her own on the table.

The CPA must pass (or have already passed) the Series 65 test. Some states will accept the passing of a combination of tests in place of the Series 65. For example, the state of Missouri accepts the combined Series 7 and Series 66 as an alternative.

Passive Ownership/Partnership

Of the three selections, passive ownership in the RIA by the CPA holds the greatest promise for firmness of commitment, privacy of involvement as a referral source, and magnitude of revenue stream endurance. (The same applies if the RIA is structured as a partnership; there is no difference between the two for the purposes of this discussion.)

The term "passive" is more significant than its core meaning of not being actively involved in the day-to-day operation of the RIA. Ownership and its status is defined in Form ADV Part I. The SEC requires owners to be placed into one of two categories: control or noncontrol. (For this writing, why change noncontrol to passive? Perception. The term "passive" helps imply nonvoting rights more than the term "noncontrol" when presenting the concept to potential CPA alliance partners.)

The SEC defines a control owner as any person or entity owning 25 percent or more of the RIA or a person holding voting power.

Points of Concern
Revenue-Sharing Rate
This is open to much contemplation and debate between the two parties and among other partners if there are any. The starting point for discussion might be that the rate should remain 15 percent. The idea here is that the strength of the passive owner position lies not in the rate of revenue sharing but in its ownership structure. A related but opposing argument might be that a higher rate will increase the ownership value of the revenue stream more quickly.

Ownership of Revenue Stream
This is the very reason for becoming an owner.

Ownership of "Booked" Referrals
In this final scenario, there is an equity structure in place to share ownership of the assets producing the management fees referred by the passive owner. However, unless the passive owner is also an IA, the passive owner is not equipped with the proper licensing to take control of the assets, or even to stake claim to them. Thus, the only circumstance under which ownership of referrals that a passive owner adds to the RIA books becomes relevant is if that passive owner becomes licensed, severs the strategic alliance, and either joins another RIA or starts his or her own. This maneuver is precisely why it is imperative that the next point of concern is heeded by the RIA.

Noncompete Agreement
The passive owner might debate that such an agreement is inappropriate because being an owner, passive or otherwise, should

preclude such restrictions. However, the alternate position would be that 1) what the passive owner might claim ownership of is a very small fraction of the total fees generated from referred clients and if the alliance ceases the proper total ownership should remain with the majority owner of the fees, and 2) if the passive owner becomes licensed and makes a move on the referred clients, he or she has violated the spirit of the strategic alliance.

Capital Contribution
The amount of money the passive owner must put on the table to become a partner is relative to two items: 1) how much money a potential full partner must put on the table, and 2) how close the amount places the passive owner to the SEC's definition of a direct owner, and thus controlling person; this amount must be added to the passive ownership value derived by some predetermined formula that accounts for the fees being generated by the clients referred through the door by the passive owner.

1 There is some logic to the conclusion that a passive partner who has yet to even refer a client should commit less (perhaps far less) than a potential partner bringing an entire, fee-generating client base to the RIA from elsewhere. These quantities are open for analysis by the owners of the RIA.

2 The amount of equity contributed by the passive owner plus the equity ownership represented by the fees generated by the referrals added to the RIA by the passive owner equals the total amount of the RIA owned by the passive owner. This number cannot rise above 25 percent. If it does, the passive owner might be passive from the RIA's perspective but is active and "in-control" from the SEC's perspective.

Shares Owned
There are a number of ways to structure stock ownership, as a few of the case studies presented in upcoming chapters show. Perhaps the simplest way to accommodate passive stock ownership is to create a second class of shares that would represent the capital contribution at one dollar per one share. If the passive owner's capital contribution

is $25,000, then 25,000 shares of that class are issued. This dollar/share ratio would remain fixed over time.

Net Ownership

This is a combination of the capital contribution and the value of the revenue stream. If the passive owner contributed $25,000 to the firm and last year received $75,000 in revenue stream, his net ownership at the close of the year is $100,000. It is this number that cannot exceed 25 percent of the total value of the firm.

Access to Financial Reporting

The CPA considering the passive owner alliance will most assuredly request examination of the financial health of the RIA. Parting with a sizeable capital contribution will most likely not—and should not—be done without thorough due diligence.

Employee Status

Probably not. Becoming an owner does not necessarily mean employment.

Voting Rights

None. Possessing the right to vote makes the owner a direct, controlling owner in the eyes of the SEC.

Legality Documentation

Legal documents defining the elements outlined here (and probably more, depending upon the situation and/or advice of counsel) should be compiled.

Tax Reporting

Partnership K-1.

Termination Provisions

The cleanest method is to impose the old "thirty-day, written notice" rule, deliverable by either party. Such a notice would trigger the buy-out provision.

Retirement Clauses

The announcement by the passive owner of retirement might be one of the reasons for the thirty-day notice.

Approval Method

This alliance is far more engaging and complex than the previous two. So if there are other owners/partners, certainly their involvement in the vetting process will be more in-depth.

Buyout Provision

This is the heart of the matter. It is essentially why the CPA becomes a passive owner. When this is invoked, the RIA buys back some multiple of the revenue stream accumulated by the passive owner. The multiple can either be fixed in the agreement or can be variable, relative to current comparative buyouts. There are, of course, numerous methods for calculating the value of the stream and for paying it out.

There are two straightforward bases for valuing the stream itself: net and gross. Net is the amount the passive owner actually receives, 15 percent of the gross. And gross is the total management fee the RIA receives from all the passive owner referrals. The question becomes, which of these numbers should be used for the basis of valuation buyout? There is some reasonable logic to using gross, in that without the passive owner alliance, the RIA firm would not have the gross stream today and therefore could not continue to enjoy it into the future, after the alliance is bought out. On the other hand, net is devoid of operational expenses. The passive owner has little if any costs associated with the revenue stream. The RIA firm does.

Estate Provision

If tragedy befalls the passive owner, the RIA firm executes the buyout provisions and funds the passive owner's estate.

Regulatory Requirements

Listing the passive owner in the ADV Part I as a direct, noncontrolling owner/partner is the sole requirement; providing the ADV Part I

In Summary

THREE COMMON AND IMPORTANT fundamentals of these three strategic alliance types are:
♦ level of commitment by both parties, more specifically by the CPA
♦ degree and method of disclosure
♦ licensing requirements

For the most part, moving from solicitor down through passive ownership, each of these fundamentals becomes more favorable:

	Commitment	Disclosure	Licensing
Solicitor	Fair	Direct/In writing	None
Investment Adviser	Good	Indirect	Yes
Passive Owner	Excellent	Unnecessary	None

to a client or potential client is unnecessary. Passive ownership in a brokerage-based RIA brought to the table by one of its RRs is simply out of the question. Because passive ownership is a subject of ADV Part I, which is not given to the client and therefore not a public disclosure matter, the issue of gaining approval from "edit-demanding" independent brokerage firms is far more cloudy. The IRR might be of the opinion that ownership is not an editable piece of data, and that the choice of business partners is of no concern to the independent brokerage.

Door Opener

The passive owner alliance is ideal as a precursor to a potential merger or acquisition between the two firms of the alliance. If an RIA and a CPA firm have some faint notion of joining forces at a later date, the passive ownership alliance provides time to see how well the two entities live together before committing to marriage.

Active Ownership/Partnership Positions

Although the passive owner/partner position outlined above brings with it a substantial measure of commitment, the active ownership position brings the ultimate dose—going into business as partners and vigorously participating in decision making and profit sharing.

Here are basic facts that pertain to regulatory registration of the RIA:

—If the RIA is an existing one, ownership changes must be made to the ADV Part I

—If the RIA is a new one, it must register as such

—If the RIA manages less than $25 million, it must register with state of domicile, if it manages more than $30 million, with the SEC, and if its assets under management fall between the two, it may register with either regulatory body.

For the sake of clarity, let's review the ownership types:

—Passive (or what the SEC calls direct, noncontrolling)

—Active (or what the SEC calls direct, controlling)

—Indirect Ownership (A note on indirect ownership—If an active owner is a business entity and not a human being, the owners of that business entity must be listed in ADV Part I as indirect owners of the RIA. Among a number of other facts, the SEC wants each of these individuals identified as a controlling or noncontrolling owner of the business entity that is an active owner of the RIA. If an owner of the business entity possesses 25 percent or more of that entity's value, that person is an indirect, controlling owner of the RIA. As well, all executive officers, partners, or directors of the business entity are indirect, controlling owners of the RIA.)

Here are basic facts that pertain to active (direct) ownership:

—The entity must be an RIA

—The SEC requires that all entities or persons be identified as direct owners on ADV Part I "that have the right to receive upon dissolution, or have contributed, 5 percent or more of the RIA's capital." *SEC Form*

ADV, Schedule A (2) (b through e). There is some question about the meaning of the term "capital." The intent of the ADV phrase above is fairly clear; however, there seems to be two potentially disparate sums of money in play: "the right to receive upon dissolution...5 percent or more of the RIA's capital" implies the proceeds from the sale of the RIA; "or have contributed, 5 percent or more of the RIA's capital" implies a capital contribution amount. These two numbers could be quite different. Five partners of an LLC might have contributed $20,000 each to get an RIA up and running, and they sell it fifteen years later for $10 million. Five percent of the initial $100,000 is $5,000. However, 5 percent of $10 million is $500,000. Unfortunately, this remains a gray area. This author contacted the SEC for clarification, but the commission declined to elaborate on this topic.

—The SEC requires that each entity or person (including executive officers, partners, and directors) with voting rights be listed as having a direct, controlling interest in the RIA

—If an owner has no voting rights *and* owns less than 25 percent of the RIA, the SEC requires that owner to be listed as a direct, non-controlling owner

—If a direct owner is a business entity, all owners possessing 25 percent or more stock in that business entity must be identified on ADV Part I as indirect, controlling owners

Following is the ownership scale as listed by the SEC on the ADV Part I:

—0 percent to less than 5 percent

—5 percent but less than 10 percent

—10 percent but less than 25 percent

—25 percent but less than 50 percent

—50 percent but less than 75 percent

—75 percent or more

Armed with these facts, fundamental decisions can now be made as to whether an active owner should be controlling or noncontrolling. If the active owner is permitted to have a 25 percent or more ownership stake, the decision has been made: controlling. If an active owner with a 2 percent stake is allowed to vote, the decision is made: controlling. An active owner with 24.9 percent stake and no voting rights is noncontrolling.

Operating Agreement

All nonregulatory points of concern are outlined in the RIA's operating agreement. Why the parties chose to share ownership and their expectations play considerable roles in defining what active ownership status they will assume in the RIA. The most common arrangement involves two existing business entities, one an RIA and the other a CPA firm. The reason each of these is at the ownership table is to share revenue and claim ownership of the revenue stream, which has value and is marketable. The expectations, on the other hand, can be a bit more complex. For example, whose revenue do they share? Under what circumstances? How much does each party receive? These and a number of other crucial topics should be detailed in the operating agreement of the strategic alliance.

Revenue Sharing

As with any small business entity, regardless of ownership makeup, there are profit and loss statements, balance sheets, stock (or shares, in the case of a partnership), and operating agreements.

The operating agreement is crucial to the success and longevity of the alliance. If the operating agreement either does not address the unique investment advisory issues or addresses them inappropriately, the alliance will self-destruct. It's essential that both parties completely understand the idiosyncrasies of compensation sharing and compliance. The best way to demonstrate this is to take a look at a real-life occurrence.

Case Study #1

The Faulty Operating Agreement of Perfect Circle Investment Advisors
Perfect Circle Investment Advisors is an SEC registered RIA located in St. Paul, Minnesota, and owned jointly by Mitchel & Pratt Investments and a single individual, James Burgess. Burgess was

also an independent registered rep (IRR) and, at the time of Perfect Circle's birth, was affiliated with Royal Alliance, an independent brokerage firm. Mitchel & Pratt Investments is wholly owned by the managing partners of Mitchel & Pratt, St. Paul's fourth-largest CPA firm, boasting roughly forty CPAs. One year after the inception of Perfect Circle Investment Advisors (PCIA), Perfect Circle Securities (PCS), at an approximate cost of $40,000, registered with the NASD as an introducing brokerage firm. Burgess moved his affiliation from Royal Alliance to PCS. The reason for creating PCS was to eliminate the 10 percent cut Royal Alliance shaved off all commissions before sending them down to Burgess and to lay the foundation for growth by adding RRs to PCS.

The ownership of both PCIA and PCS was split right down the middle between Mitchel & Pratt Investments (MPI) and Burgess. PCIA was presented to the public as a division of Mitchel & Pratt, CPAs (M&P). The intent of creating Perfect Circle was to build a thriving investment advisory division of M&P by entering into various strategic alliances with other financial entities, as well as by recruiting RRs to affiliate with Perfect Circle Securities.

The operating agreement was written to the best of both parties' abilities and reflected their knowledge of the intricacies of the investment world. For a few years, all went well. Then, because of poorly conceived and written clauses within the operating agreement, outside influences necessary for growth and operational efficiency applied strain to the alliance. When examined closely, the operating agreement actually prevented growth as it was intended—through alliances and by accumulating a herd of producing RRs. In both cases, there simply was not sufficient revenue to share with either alliance partners or RRs, both of which could cut better strategic alliance deals elsewhere. The revenue-sharing clauses in Perfect Circle's operating agreement laid a heavy burden on its competitive position in attracting growth opportunities.

Finally, six years after inception, the issue of how a rather large compensation check from a Burgess client obtained prior to the creation of Perfect Circle should be shared with MPI was not clearly defined in the operating agreement and sparks flew. M&P withheld referrals, and the alliance that had began with so much promise six years earlier ground to a standstill. The lofty ambitions for Perfect Circle's creation were doomed the moment the operating agreement was signed.

A year later Perfect Circle reported a change in ownership on its ADV Part I from 50 percent MPI and 50 percent James Burgess to varying ownership levels by Perfect Circle's five executive officers, including James Burgess. (The aggressive growth and expansion plans of the "new" Perfect Circle, and its operating agreement, which fosters such growth, is the subject of another case study.)

The problem clauses in Perfect Circle's operating agreement:
The revenue/cost structure looked like this:

Gross Profit:	**100.0%**
Referrer Fee:	10.0%
Relationship Manager:	25.0%
Operating Expenses:	50.0%
Net Profit:	**15.0%**
Net to MPI—	7.5%
Net to Burgess—	7.5%

The referrer fee went directly to either Mitchel & Pratt Investments or Burgess, whichever brought the client through the door. The relationship manager at Perfect Circle is the licensed individual who is directly responsible for client satisfaction in every respect. Once a client is satisfactorily in the door, the relationship manager assumes control of the case. Perfect Circle's philosophy is to provide intense service, so operating expenses were higher than most investment advisory firms; they oscillated between 45 percent and 55 percent. One hundred percent of the net profit was split fifty-fifty between Mitchel & Pratt Investments and James Burgess.

Flaws in developing strategic alliances between Perfect Circle and other referrers:
An immediate observation is that there is precious little left in the above cost structure from which to pay other professional referrers.

Schwab Institutional requests 15 percent of the ongoing asset management fee on clients it refers to RIAs within its system. If one accepts this as an industry norm, the other referrers deserve 15 percent. Once the other referrer firm is contentedly within Perfect Circle's system, a relationship manager is assigned, thereby accounting for his 25 percent to manage the new client. Holding operating expenses dead center within its fluctuation band, Perfect Circle's net profit has diminished to 10 percent, 5 percent to MPI and 5 percent to Burgess. Of course, if operating expenses move toward its high side, net profit sinks even lower.

Here's the revised, most ominous look:

Gross Profit:	**100.0%**
Other Referrer's Fee:	15.0%
Relationship Manager:	25.0%
Operating Expenses:	55.0%
Net Profit:	**5.0%**
Net to MPI—	2.5%
Net to Burgess—	2.5%

Flaws in recruiting RRs and IAs to Perfect Circle:

Forty percent is about the lowest payout for RRs employed by brokerage firms. The highest, roughly 90 percent, is paid out by independent brokerage firms. The lowest fee rate for IAs using a brokerage firm's RIA is 85 percent. The highest is 100 percent, captured by the autonomous unassociated RIA.

As noted above, the relationship manager payout at Perfect Circle is 25 percent. The 15 percent difference relative to the lowest RR payout of 40 percent is only slightly outweighed by the relationship manager's exposure to the potential quantity and quality of clients MPI delivers. (When MPI, as a result of the disputed revenue, shut down the referral spigot, the "potential" quantity dried up and the relationship manager's slight advantage converted to a massive disadvantage, creating further pressure within Perfect Circle to pull out of the partnership.) Adding insult to injury, the relationship manager did not even receive the 10 percent referrer fee (outlined on page 77) when he brought in a client by his own efforts. That fell to Perfect Circle's bottom line and was gobbled up by the two owners. These paltry conditions presented little motivation for an RR or IA practicing elsewhere to jump ship and climb aboard Perfect Circle.

In addition, if an RR or IA joined Perfect Circle, it was required he sell his book of business to Perfect Circle at a discounted revenue-flow rate. The discount was justified by 1) the higher quality of service delivered to the RR/IA clients and 2) the reduction in time the RR/IA had to devote to that service. (At the time of Perfect Circle's demise, it had one relationship manager. During entry negotiations, he refused to sell his business. Perfect Circle, in an effort to at least prime the empire-building pump, acquiesced.)

The gray accounting of future revenue from Burgess's pre-Perfect Circle clients:

The day Perfect Circle was created it was devoid of clients. However, this was not the case with James Burgess's practice prior to joining Mitchel & Pratt, CPAs, in the new venture. Burgess, practicing for over twenty years, had constructed a vigorous and potent fee-based business.

The revenues generated by these clients were only partially isolated in the primary calculation of how the revenues of Perfect Circle were to be shared by MPI and Burgess. This small exposure caused profit to be elevated on the secondary calculation scale, thereby creating the conflict that ultimately broke the back of the partnership. Here's what happened:

Primary calculation:

That portion of Perfect Circle's profit attributed solely to Burgess equaled his pre-Perfect Circle client revenues minus expenses attributed to those revenues. The crucial phrase that caused the controversy is "expenses attributed." We'll get to this in a minute.

Secondary calculation:

All profit of Perfect Circle was allocated to Burgess and MPI by the following revenue volume scale:

		Burgess/MPI
1	$0 to $500,000	70/30
2	$500,001 to $1,000,000	65/35
3	$1,000,001 to $1,500,000	62/38
4	$1,500,001 to $2,000,000	58/42
5	In excess of $2,000,001	55/45

The revenue occurrence in question was a 1035 exchange of five variable annuities from a life insurance company that was experiencing regulatory problems to a variable annuity company in good shape. The commission (thru Perfect Circle Securities) was slightly over $600,000. All other revenue for Perfect Circle during that year totaled $710,000, against expenses of $335,000.

The primary point of contention between Burgess and MPI was how expenses would be attributed to the single $600,000 revenue event.

Burgess's stance:

The amount of administrative effort involved in preparation of five annuity applications and ancillary documentation was negligible, a "nonevent" for expense purposes. Therefore, in determining the allocation scale level, the $600,000 of annuity commission should be excluded from profit, creating the following calculation:

$710,000 of revenue

− $335,000 of expenses

_____

$375,000 of distributable profit

This profit amount occupies level 1 on the allocation scale, distributing $262,500 (70 percent) to Burgess and $112,500 (30 percent) to MPI.

Burgess net income: $600,000 plus $262,500 equals $862,500. MPI net income: $112,500.

MPI's stance:

Not fully comprehending the simplicity of completing annuity applications, MPI argued that because the revenue generated was so high, the amount of time to produce it had to be positively correlated. It insisted that the expenses of $335,000 be applied against the entire revenue amount of $1,310,000 ($710,000 plus $600,000) of that year, creating the following calculation:

$1,310,000 of revenue
− $ 335,000 of expenses
_____
$ 975,000 of distributable profit

This profit amount vaults to level 2 on the allocation scale, distributing $633,750 (65 percent) to Burgess and $341,250 (35 percent) to MPI.

Burgess net income: $633,750.
MPI net income: $341,250.

Net income difference between stances:
Burgess a negative $228,750.
MPI a positive $228,750.

Conclusion

The magnitude of the differences makes it apparent how this particular instance collapsed the partnership. Operating agreements cannot address and neutralize every eventuality waiting to trip them up. But when a strategic alliance between two pre-existing, clearly distinctive entities is under consideration, every imaginable nuance—especially those involving money—should be examined from all directions.

The "letter" of the operating agreement does not side with James Burgess. The definition outlining the allocation of expenses is clear: total expenses against total revenue. Mr. Burgess would have been wise to insert clarity on this eventuality in the operating agreement from the outset. Twenty years in the profession is ample experience to inform him that just such a windfall occasion from a pre-Perfect Circle client would probably occur and failing to prepare for it in the operating agreement was a significant oversight.

The "spirit" of the operating agreement does not side with MPI. Business rationality should prevail if partnerships are worthwhile. CPAs must gain a complete understanding of financial services intricacies because it is the industry in which the strategic alliance operates. To conclude that the cost of administrative preparation of five annuity contracts equaled $228,750 demonstrates MPI's lack of business judgment and industry-specific knowledge.

Breaching both the letter and the spirit of the agreement fatally wounded the partnership. It was avoidable.

The Case for an Arbitrator Clause

The collision between the "letter" and the "spirit" interpretations propelled the controversy into the emotional arena. Once trapped there, only dollar signs mattered. The "letter" meant nothing. The "spirit" meant nothing. The $228,750 meant everything. Attempted compromises only weakened the trust that once bound the partnership.

While developing the operating agreement, had the two parties realized disagreements borne not only of a lack of understanding of the investment world but also of unforeseen twists could arise, they might well have inserted an arbitrator clause.

Ownership of the Revenue Stream

Owners of an RIA, in reality, own nothing. What is perceived to be owned are the assets that produce the streaming asset management fees. In reality, the owners of the RIA have no legal claim to those assets. Their clients own them. An RIA can be generating $1 million of annual fees on $100 million of client assets it manages; the RIA owners can purport to own $1 million of revenue. The next day, all the RIA clients move their assets elsewhere, and the owners now own nothing. This is a stark interpretation of RIA ownership value, but it could become, to some degree, reality.

In only two circumstances does this perception of ownership of an RIA take on meaning: when the RIA is sold or when it alters its ownership structure under strain. If an RIA is sold and the transition is smooth, the clients will be inclined to leave their fee-generating assets with the new owners. If the RIA modifies its ownership due to friction, clients will fall into one of four categories:

♦ **unaffected**—those that will remain with the RIA

♦ **nervous**—those that are anxious about the instability of the RIA

♦ **departing**—those that will leave on their own and go to other investment sources
♦ **following**—those that will follow the departing owners to new investment sources

This volatility in client posture diminishes, or at the very least calls into question, the value of the RIA. It is during these times that the owners of an RIA are reminded of how fragile the value of the RIA really is and who actually owns the assets that generate the revenue.

Uncommon Active Ownership Arrangement

Owning 25 percent or more of an RIA and not holding voting rights makes the owner direct and controlling (active, for our purposes). Not maintaining voting rights implies the owner is not involved in the daily operation of the RIA and has simply infused money into it at some point. The purposes for doing this vary, but the primary reason is as an investment, much as one would invest in any other small business. But considering the dialogue above regarding the stability of the only asset of value an RIA possesses, this type of ownership would be tenuous and unusual.

In Summary

The facts we know about RIAs:
—They are regulated by the 1940 Act
—They receive fees directly from a client
—Their primary means of disclosure is the ADV Part II
—They can be a dual, that is, a registered rep and an RIA
—If they manage over $30 million they register with the SEC, less than $25 million they register with their state of domicile, and between with whichever body they choose.

RIAs: Brokerage-Based and Autonomous

Brokerage-based: owned and controlled by national or regional independent or employer brokerage firm.

Autonomous associated: owned and controlled by an independent RR or group of independent RRs so they can offer fee-based advice.

Autonomous unassociated: owned and controlled by a person or group who are not members of the NASD.

Dissecting Services and Their Fees

Fee-Only: The adviser receives fees for work done and services provided to clients.

Fee-Based: The adviser receives fees for client services, but may also receive commission or other compensation on the sale of products.

Assets Under Management: There are varying degrees of asset management style. The simplest, least active is to buy positions in a client's portfolio, hold and monitor them, changing very infrequently. Alternately, an RIA can offer clients literally any related financial service.

Investment Policies: An investment policy is an RIA's method of managing its clients' assets. Investment policies can contort into many different forms employing up to five layers of professional service: the RIA itself, the institutional brokerage, a platform service, third-party managers, and institutional managers.

Management Variations:

Internal/Specific—The RIA manages client portfolios using individual equities

Internal/General—The RIA manages client portfolios using third-party managers

External/Specific—The RIA relinquishes management of client portfolios to institutional managers

The Variables—Annuities and Life Insurance: The "freedom to walk" concept is much the same in variable life insurance. The surrender penalty of traditional variable life insurance does not exist in no-commission insurance, where the cash value and surrender value are the same from the outset.

Fees—Who Charges Whom for What:

Internal/Specific—Institutional brokerage from client account to the RIA

Internal/General—Platform from institutional brokerage account to RIA and to third-party manager

External/Specific—Institutional manager from institutional account to RIA

Variable Annuities and Life Insurance—through the client's institutional brokerage account or directly from the client

Built-in Vessels for Alliances

There are three general methods of crafting strategic alliances already built into the framework of the 1940 Act and subsequent SEC rulings over the years: solicitor's agreement, investment adviser, passive ownership. There are numerous areas of concerns shared among the three, the answers to which can vary from one method to another.

♦ Revenue-Sharing Rate
♦ Ownership of Revenue Stream
♦ Ownership of "Booked" Referrals
♦ Noncompete Agreement
♦ Capital Contribution
♦ Shares Owned
♦ Net Ownership
♦ Access to Financial Reporting
♦ Employee Status
♦ Voting Rights
♦ Legality Documentation
♦ Tax Reporting
♦ Termination Provisions
♦ Retirement Clauses (Trigger and Payout Period)
♦ Approval Method
♦ Buyout Provision
♦ Estate Provision
♦ Regulatory Requirements

Solicitor's Agreement

The CPA can be a human being or a business entity. The solicitor's agreement legally appoints the CPA as an associate of the RIA. Prior to signing investment advisory agreements, the client must sign and be given a copy of a disclosure document, which outlines the arrangement between the solicitor and the RIA.

Investment Adviser

An Investment Adviser (IA) comes in two forms: on-site and off-site. The on-site IA is actively engaged in the pursuit of clients and regards the position as full time. The off-site IA has no permanent presence within the RIA's offices, pursues clients only occasionally, and works part time.

Passive Ownership/Partnership

Passive ownership by a CPA firm in an RIA is firmer in commitment, more private, and provides an enduring payout. The term "passive" is more significant than its core meaning of not being actively involved in the day-to-day operation of the RIA.

In Summary

	Commitment	Disclosure	Licensing
Solicitor	Fair	Direct/In writing	None
Investment Adviser	Good	Indirect	Yes
Passive Owner	Excellent	Unnecessary	None

Active Ownership/Partnership Positions

Here are basic facts that pertain to active (direct) ownership:

—the entity must be an RIA

—the SEC requires that all entities or persons be identified as direct owners on ADV Part I

—the SEC requires that each entity or person (including executive officers, partners, and directors) with voting rights be listed as having a direct, controlling interest in the RIA

—if an owner has no voting rights and owns less than 25 percent of the RIA, the SEC requires that owner be listed as a direct, non-controlling owner

—if a direct owner is a business entity, all owners possessing 25 percent or more of that entity must be identified on ADV Part I as indirect, controlling owners

Most Common Active Ownership Arrangement
The most common arrangement involves two existing business entities, one an RIA and the other a CPA firm partnership. The reason each of these is at the ownership table is to share revenue and claim ownership of the revenue stream, which has value and is marketable.

Operating Agreement—Revenue Sharing
The operating agreement is crucial to the success and longevity of the alliance. If the operating agreement either does not address the unique investment advisory issues or addresses them inappropriately, the alliance will self-destruct.

Case Study #1: The faulty operating agreement of Perfect Circle Investment Advisors.
Their operating agreement prevented growth as intended, through alliances and accumulating a herd of producing RRs. In addition, allocation of a huge revenue check generated by one owner's pre-Perfect Circle clients caused strain and finally the demise of the partnership, which might have been avoided had they included an arbitration clause in the operating agreement.

Ownership—Revenue Stream
Client assets produce management fee revenue, which is of value and sellable. In reality, the owners of an RIA have no legal claim to client assets. The clients own them, which makes the value of the revenue source somewhat dubious.

Uncommon Active Ownership Arrangement
Owning 25 percent or more of an RIA and not holding voting rights.

In the next chapter, the pertinent daily compliance obligations of both RRs and RIAs are dissected.

5 | Compliance

Compliance is different from satisfying the regulatory mechanisms of the NASD and SEC that allow entry into the investment advisory profession. Compliance is an ongoing series of tasks. For an investment adviser who is a registered representative (RR), these duties are multitudinous and daily. For a registered investment adviser (RIA), they are fewer and less burdensome. Although there are many components of compliance, there are four that eat annoyingly into the wallet and the schedule: process and procedures, errors and omissions (E&O) insurance, training and education (T&E), and audits.

Registered Representatives

Registered reps must abide by all parts of the Securities Act of 1934 and the rules and regulations the NASD and SEC have adopted since its passage in the early 1930s.

Process and Procedures

The heart of process and procedures is paper. Forms and written communications. Many of each. The reason for this strict process flow of paperwork is to maintain compliance controls and to document and record those controls for review by the compliance official of a branch office. All forms must be completed in their entirety or they need to take a return trip to the RR who put them into the process. If the CPA firm is a satellite of an established branch office, all paperwork must flow back to the branch office.

Below are the forms and means of communication that typically consume the most time and oversight when moving through the office:

New Brokerage or Mutual Fund Account Application

This opens the client account either at the brokerage firm with which the RR is affiliated or directly at the mutual fund family. The account application is the father to all the other forms. Without it, none of the others are needed and to it, all the others are attached. Every completed new account application is logged into the daily log binder or file with the RR identification number, client name, and account type (joint, IRA, etc.). Sometime during the business day, the compliance officer reviews, approves, and signs all new account applications and the associated, attached forms. Copies are made of the application and all associated documents, and they are date-stamped and placed in the client's master file. The paperwork packet is then sent to the brokerage firm or the mutual fund family.

Many brokerage firms now provide their RRs with Internet access to blank new account applications, where all the data can be entered. This method ensures that RRs, most of whom are notoriously horrible at paperwork, complete the entire form; the software will not allow the RR to print off the application until all fields are finished. The printed form still needs the client's review and signature.

Explanation of Investment (EOI)

The EOI provides the client with five specific pieces of information about the nature of the investments being offered: the client's investment goals, the value of the shares being bought, the reduced sales charge notice, the clarification of distributions notice, and the cost of purchase details. The client checks or initials each data point and signs the document along with the RR.

Client's Investment Goals

Most brokerage firms have standard EOI forms they supply to their RRs. Most EOIs ask the client to check any of the following investment goals that apply: aggressive growth, moderate growth, conservative growth/income, long-term income, preservation of capital, or tax advantage. The purpose of this question is to record for file purposes the risk profile to which the client has agreed.

Value of Shares

This gives notice that the client recognizes that the value of the mutual fund or annuity shares can go up and down.

Reduced Sales Charge

This alerts the client to two potentially favorable concepts: breakpoints and letters of intent. The RR often (and unfortunately, sometimes intentionally) does not explain these options to clients. Breakpoints refer to a reduced front load sales charge when specific amounts are invested in a lump sum in the same fund family. Clients can also take advantage of breakpoints by signing a letter of intent, which states they will invest a specific amount over the next few months that would qualify for breakpoints intended for a lump sum investment. By making this a notice on the EOI, the RR must explain the concepts.

Clarification of Distributions

This lets the client know that there is no advantage to buying mutual fund shares right before a capital gains or dividend distribution announcement. (In fact, as advisers know, there is a significant disadvantage to doing so. Because the gains in a fund accumulate all year, and the firm's net asset value reflects those gains, if you buy fund shares immediately before the annual dividend distribution, you're paying for those gains, only to have them immediately returned to you as a taxable distribution.)

Cost of Purchase

This informs the client of the share type (A, B, or C) being purchased and the percentage sales charge being levied, whether up front or as a result of a contingent deferred sales charge.

Switch Letter

A switch letter is used when an RR is moving money from one mutual fund to another. It is required whether the move is for an existing client or a new client. The switch letter indicates what fund is being liquidated, the date it was purchased, and the cost in dollars to the client at the time. It then requires the name of the fund being bought and the cost to the client in dollars. It also establishes the client's investment goal.

The purpose of this document is fairly evident: to prevent the churning of mutual fund shares.

Automated Customer Account Transfer (ACAT)

ACAT is an acronym for automated customer account transfer. It is the name for the central clearing house that the standardized ACAT form moves through and that carries out the transfer of an investor's money from one brokerage firm to another. If a client wants to move his investments from the control of an RR at Merrill Lynch to the control of an RR at Royal Alliance, an ACAT is completed and signed by the client. Both brokerage firms honor the ACAT form and execute the transfer of funds. Without a properly completed ACAT, client assets will not be moved. ACATs are copied and included in the client's master file; the original is attached to the new account application and sent to the RR's brokerage firm.

Automatic Clearing House (ACH)

An ACH form executes the automatic and regular transfer of funds to or from a brokerage account or bank account. If, for example, a retired client needs a specific monthly amount from his brokerage investments to maintain his lifestyle, an ACH is completed to facilitate an automatic transfer of funds from the brokerage account on a given day every month to the client's checking account.

Client Securities-Related Communications

Registered reps communicate with clients and potential clients in two ways: marketing/advertising and personal correspondence—via mail, e-mail, or oral communication. Those CPAs unfamiliar with the investment profession (and many RRs unfamiliar with the fundamental rules) will find the regulations dictating procedures for client communications, especially personal securities-related correspondence, to be extraordinarily intrusive. However, because the NASD is charged with protecting the public from unscrupulous boasting (or outright lying), it demands that its members abide by stringent surveillance procedures.

All marketing/advertising material must be submitted to the branch office compliance officer (commonly referred to as the ME, managing executive), who, in turn, submits the material to the brokerage firm compliance department for approval. Each piece of communication is assigned an approval code, and some brokerage firms require that code be recorded somewhere on the marketing/advertising piece itself.

An RR's communication with clients and potential clients is a mutual exercise, conducted by both sides, orally and in writing. The only method reviewed, copied, and filed is written correspondence—letters or e-mails. From a compliance perspective, both are identical.

Incoming securities-related correspondence (sent to the RR from the outside) is opened, reviewed, and initialed by the branch office compliance officer. The purpose of this exercise is to detect complaints against an RR, unauthorized outside business activity in which an RR might be engaging, or any RR activity that violates NASD rules. This, of course, means that private mail sent by clients to the RR is opened and read by individuals to whom the letter is not addressed. Each piece of correspondence is copied before delivery to the RR, and numbered and filed. That file is almost always reviewed during audits.

Outgoing securities-related correspondence does not leave the branch office without review and approval by the compliance officer. All outbound correspondence is also numbered and filed.

Managing the flow of correspondence that is touchable is simple.

Doing so with e-mail is not quite as easy, but e-mail is regarded as correspondence and falls within the same control, review, and approval guidelines as paper mail. Branch office compliance officers can require that all RRs under its supervision, inside the branch office or as members of a satellite office, send copies of securities-related e-mails to a compliance mailbox for review before they are sent to their final destination. Because of the simplicity and ease of sending and receiving e-mails, firms have had difficulty getting RRs to actually adhere to this requirement. (There is software available to compliance officers that automatically captures e-mails from RRs and delivers it to a specified compliance mailbox. You can find one at www.compliancecompany.com.)

Errors & Omissions (E&O) Insurance

The cost of E&O insurance has increased dramatically over the past few years, and it has become an important compliance expense factor. E&O insurance falls within the compliance category because brokerage firms will not allow the affiliation of RRs unless the RR has E&O insurance.

The cost of E&O insurance depends on three major characteristics of the individual RR: the geographic market of the RR's practice, the number of years in practice, and the RR's integrity history. An RR who has just been released from prison for fraud and starts a new practice in Manhattan can expect to pay more for E&O insurance than an RR with an immaculate twenty-five-year track record operating in Omaha, Nebraska. In the mainstream, however, current annual premiums range from $1,000 to $2,500.

Training and Education (T&E)

Training and education is not the same as continuing education. Continuing education is a discretionary exercise in which each RR participates. T&E consists of two tests, or elements, both mandated by the NASD: the regulatory element and the firm element.

The regulatory element focuses on issues involving ethics, compliance and regulation, and RR sales practices. RRs cannot fail the three-hour regulatory element test. Questions are posed on scenarios presented. The RR must provide a suitable proportion of correct answers within each scenario module before being allowed to progress to the next one. The RR is required to take the regulatory element on or about his second anniversary of becoming a member of the NASD and every three years thereafter.

The firm element is directed by the RR's brokerage. The brokerage firm itself decides on the content of the test based on its unique business practices. As with the regulatory element, the firm element is a no-fail test. Most brokerage firms require their RRs to take this test once a year.

Also falling into the T&E category is the annual compliance meeting that all RRs are required to attend. The compliance officer at the branch office normally conducts these meetings. All RRs operating in satellite offices must attend. At the annual compliance meeting, all new compliance issues are reviewed and RRs are required to indicate in writing participation in any business outside the securities profession. (Even if an RR is paid to flip hamburgers at her mother's restaurant, she must list this as an outside business activity.)

Audits

Brokerage firm compliance departments are required to perform annual on-site audits of all branch offices, conducted by the compliance officer of the branch. These audits are usually scheduled in advance; however, the brokerage firm's compliance officer can stroll in unannounced. Here's a sampling of those general procedure items examined:

♦ Incoming correspondence file
♦ Outgoing correspondence file
♦ Bank statements for the past twelve months
♦ Deposit records
♦ Client complaint file
♦ Signature guarantee log file
♦ Current do-not-call list
♦ Checks and securities received log
♦ Checkbook
♦ Canceled checks

In addition, the auditors will request to examine the master client files of a randomly selected list of clients. They will then scrutinize the content of the files to ensure that all applicable documents are present and completed properly.

In addition to the general office files, the auditors will inspect the material the branch compliance officer is responsible for maintaining, such as the:

♦ Private security transaction file
♦ Advertising/sales literature file (business cards, stationery, etc.)
♦ Personnel file for each RR
♦ Supervisory client files
♦ Request for an approval of an outside activity file (the RR's participation in business activities outside the securities profession)
♦ Supervisory logs for the past twelve months
♦ Transaction log file for each RR

And finally, the auditors will zero in on specific RR client files, inspecting the:

♦ Product cross-reference file
♦ Customer account statements
♦ Approval for any outside activities
♦ Client transaction logs

If a CPA firm is a satellite office, attached to a branch office, the compliance officer of the branch is required to perform the exact same functions at the satellite (except compliance officer files). The brokerage auditors will in turn review the content and results of these audits.

In addition, RR branch offices are subject to unannounced audits by either the NASD or authorities from the state of residence.

Registered Investment Advisers

Because, in essence, an RIA is self-regulated in that its doctrine for behavior is its own Form ADV (compiled according to the requirements of the Investment Advisers Act of 1940), and because RIA work is fee-based, compliance issues are miniscule compared to those of the RR.

Process and Procedures

The internal office procedures for opening a new account are quite similar to those of an RR branch office, with a few notable exceptions. For example, the procedures that an RIA follows when client assets are sold and new shares bought are very different than those an RR follows when current client assets are realigned.

New Brokerage or Mutual Fund Account Application

An RIA never places client assets directly with a mutual fund family because, among other things, mutual fund families are not equipped to deduct asset management fees from client accounts; therefore, a specific mutual fund application is unnecessary. Instead, assets are placed with an institutional brokerage firm, which, in turn, buys shares of a mutual fund for a client's account. But institutional brokerage account applications require all the same information required by a retail account application being filled out in an RR branch office. And, as with the RR, they must be completed thoroughly and properly before they are accepted by the brokerage firm, and probably before they make it out of the RIA office itself.

Explanation of Investment (EOI)

Because these provide commission information to clients on the sale and purchase of mutual funds, they are irrelevant to an RIA practice.

Switch Letter

These are also unnecessary. As already mentioned, this form is used to alert the client of any commission imbalances when mutual fund shares are sold and the proceeds used to purchase others. Because the RIA works for a fee, the movement of assets is a noncost activity to the client and therefore the client doesn't need to be alerted to the potential monetary setbacks of these moves.

Automated Customer Account Transfer (ACAT)

The RIA uses the ACAT in the same way the RR does. It's a mechanism to standardize the movement of investment assets from one brokerage firm to another. The investment adviser's method of compensation has no bearing on whether the ACAT is used.

Automatic Clearing House (ACH)

As is the case with the ACAT, there is no difference in how RIAs and RRs use the ACH.

Client Securities-Related Communications

The 1940 Act gives RIAs no prescribed process for communicating with clients—unlike the directions the NASD gives to its RRs. However, in two sections of the 1940 Act, it is made quite clear that fabrications of any sort are forbidden.

Section 207, Material Misstatements, provides that "It shall be unlawful for any person willfully to make any untrue statement of a material fact in any registration application or report filed with the Commission … or willfully to omit to state in any such application or report any material fact which is required to be stated therein." This applies to the ADV Part II, as a means of communication with clients.

Section 204, Reports by Investment Advisers, states "Every investment adviser who makes use of the mails or of any means or instrumentality of interstate commerce in connection with his or its business as an investment adviser … shall make and keep for prescribed periods such records …, furnish such copies thereof, and make and disseminate such reports as the Commission, by rule, may prescribe as necessary or appropriate in the public interest or for the protection of investors. All records (as so defined) of such investment advisers are subject at any time, or from time to time, to such reasonable periodic, special, or other examinations by representatives of the Commission as the Commission deems necessary or appropriate in the public interest or for the protection of investors."

Furthermore, in a letter published by the SEC in May of 2000 highlighting common discrepancies found during audits of RIAs, the notion of "duty to disclose" in communication with clients was addressed.

> Advisers are required to disclose any facts that might cause the adviser to render advice that is not disinterested. When an adviser fails to disclose information regarding potential conflicts of interest, clients are unable to make informed decisions about entering into or continuing the advisory relationship.
>
> During inspections, the examination staff reviews an adviser's filings with the Commission and other materials provided to clients to ensure that the adviser's disclosures are accurate, timely, and do not omit material information. Examples of failures to disclose material information to clients would include:
>
> An adviser fails to disclose all fees that a client would pay in connection with the advisory contract, including how fees are charged, and whether fees are negotiable;
>
> An adviser fails to disclose its affiliation with a broker-dealer or other securities professionals or issuers; and
>
> An adviser with discretionary assets under management fails to disclose that it is in a precarious financial condition that is likely to impair its ability to meet contractual commitments to clients.

Errors and Omissions (E&O) Insurance

Errors and omissions insurance is not typically needed by an RIA that serves individual clients. An RIA's ADV Part II reveals all the necessary detail of how the RIA operates and an RIA's investment policy agreement, signed by the client, outlines the investment methodology the client can expect; errors or omissions would occur in the content of these documents. Errors or omissions, therefore, occur when an act is performed that is either not disclosed in or is different from these documents.

If an RIA ventures into the institutional market, those institutions will more than likely require the RIA to carry E&O insurance.

Training and Education (T&E)

There are no mandatory training or education requirements, at either the state or the SEC level.

Audits

The entity under which an RIA is registered, either the state of domicile or the SEC, can conduct unannounced audits during business hours. Usually, however, each body schedules such audits well in advance. It also typically provides a list of documents it will review. All such documents and policies and procedures are compared against the RIA's ADV.

The next chapter takes us deeply into the details of an RR/CPA alliance.

6 | CPAs and Registered Representatives (RRs)

Certified public accountant entities range from a sole proprietor working out of the home to an international monolith. This analysis does not venture into the monolith territory. It begins with the one-person practice and ends with the local CPA firm with a handful of partners and a few dozen employees. It is far easier to engage in a strategic alliance with an investment adviser when decision making is self-contained and relatively quick. Remember the core reason for a strategic alliance: to share in the revenue of the investment adviser, either directly or indirectly. Let's review the RR profile.

Types of Registered Representatives

1   Employed (ERR)—the RR a) works for the brokerage firm with which he is affiliated, b) is responsible for little if any overhead cost to operate his practice, and c) experiences an average payout of 40 percent to 50 percent on product sales.

2   Independent (IRR)—the RR a) affiliates with a brokerage firm that is a vendor to the RR's business and can be fired, b) is responsible for all operational expenses, and c) realizes an average payout of 85 percent on product sales.

Registered Rep Strategic Alliance Choices

In forming a strategic alliance, a CPA could:

1 become an RR with an existing employed RR (ERR)
2 become an RR with an existing independent RR (IRR)
3 lease office space to an RR (more than likely an IRR)
4 provide professional consulting services to an RR (more than likely an IRR)
5 engage in any legal combination of the above, yielding nine potential choices (one cannot engage in No. 1 and No. 2 simultaneously).

For each of these choices, the following fifteen factors that will assist the CPA in formulating a decision about which choice best fits which entity are examined:

1 **Regulatory/licensing requirements:** What is required of the CPA firm by law to engage in this alliance?

2 **Method of compensation:** How is the CPA firm compensated, and is this method negotiable?

3 **Potential compensation amount:** How much compensation can the CPA expect, relative to the other choices for strategic alliances?

4 **Compliance:** What daily compliance issues, if any, does the CPA firm face and at roughly what cost?

5 **Office logistics:** Where must the CPA firm be located to legally do business in the strategic alliance?

6 **Client profile:** How does the typical client profile match up with each alliance choice?

7 **Current entity size:** Is the size of the CPA firm of any importance in choosing a strategic alliance structure?

8 **Current entity business structure:** Likewise, does the CPA firm's current business structure affect which alliance choice is best?

9 **Shared-compensation flow inside the CPA firm:** What happens with the alliance revenue once it gets inside the CPA firm?

10 **Internal marketing among CPA partners, managers, and others:** What are the best methods for rallying the troops around the alliance?

11 Managing clients' perceptions of the alliance: What is the best way to present the new alliance to the CPA's client base?

12 Marketing to clients (current and future): What marketing techniques work best?

13 CPAs as the "Client Advocate": Can the CPA ethically claim to sit on the same side of the table as the client and opposite the RR alliance partner?

14 Evolutionary prognosis: What might each alliance type look like in the future and why will it take its shape?

15 If needed, an honorable dissolution: How to escape cleanly and honorably from the alliance.

Some of the fifteen factors will have little or no impact on a few of the nine choices. Some of the fifteen factors will have an identical impact on a few of the nine choices. When this occurs, the identical choices are identified and the previous entry is summarized. If they are somewhat identical, they are identified, the previous entry is summarized, and the nuanced differences are examined.

Many of the fifteen factors should not be presented in isolation from investment adviser perceptions regarding particular factors and their impact on the investment adviser's practice. In other words, what does the other side of the fence have to say about a particular factor within a certain alliance choice? Comments and opinions that advisers might offer about the various factors are presented under the heading "Investment Adviser's Comment."

Becoming a Registered Rep With an Existing Employed Registered Rep

Regulatory/Licensing Requirements

Become a member of the NASD and an employee of the ERR's affiliated brokerage firm. Pass the Series 6 test to sell mutual funds and variable annuities or pass the Series 7 test to sell all individual equities, including those covered by the Series 6 examination.

INVESTMENT ADVISER'S COMMENT

I certainly don't want to eliminate myself as a potential alliance partner with you, but in all fairness, if you go through all this licensing and affiliation with my employer brokerage, why do you need me? Do it yourself. The only thing I bring to the table is a wealth of experience, product knowledge, and expertise on managing documentation (and there are a whole lot of documents). If you think you can learn quickly and manage these with your clients and prospects, go for it ... alone.

Method of Compensation

As a member of the NASD and an employee of the ERR's brokerage firm, the CPA is paid on commission, and receives an average of 45 percent of all commission generated from sales. The CPA receives a unique RR identification number assigned by the brokerage firm. This number is necessary to receive commission; it is combined with the number of the RR with whom the CPA is aligning, to create a "group" number, also assigned by the brokerage firm. This group (the CPA and the ERR) receives commission on all joint sales, and that commission is split by the percentage agreed upon by the strategic alliance members.

CPAs work on an hourly or project basis, not on commission. So this RR arrangement is different from what an accountant is accustomed to. For some CPAs, this might be a basic philosophical dilemma they must solve when considering this and other strategic alliance options.

INVESTMENT ADVISER'S COMMENT

Here's the good news: as an employed RR, I've got a big name behind me, such as Morgan Stanley, AG Edwards, Merrill Lynch, or one of many others. Your clients will bask in the warmth of the marketing goodies of these monikers: trust, integrity, performance, et cetera. These are quality selling points, which make you look good.

Here's the not-so-good news: There's a cost to this high-profile luster. As an employed registered rep, my payout is roughly net 50 percent of the commission on the sale of mutual funds, annuities, and life insurance. Net is my average annual payout percent, which starts at 40 percent on

January 1st of every year and increases throughout the year based on the amount of sales I produce. If I have a good year, I can get up to a 60 percent net payout level. In an average year, I'll hit the 50 percent net level. The payout on individual securities commission is only slightly lower.

So here's my take of our commission in an alliance: Right up front we forfeit to the house (our employer brokerage firm) about 50 percent. So if we sell $50,000 of Class A mutual fund shares with a 5 percent front load, we'll get half that, or $1,250. If our strategic alliance split is fifty-fifty, we each get $625. Now I'm not one to claim that as chicken feed, but most of the work in landing the sale will come from me via my expertise, my knowledge and explanation of the product and the subsequent documentation, as well as my ability to move the client through our system. In effect, I'll do most of the heavy lifting. So I'll have to move forward with a strategic alliance split not of fifty-fifty but of seventy/thirty, which, in the example above, means you get $375 and I get $875. That's for the delivery of the client's name and perhaps your token appearance at the introduction meeting.

Potential Compensation Amount

Very low.

Compliance

As with any RR, the CPA agrees to abide by all the rules and regulations of the brokerage firm's best practices manual, which may be more stringent than those of the NASD. The NASD or the brokerage firm requires the RR to complete annual continuing education courses.

Office Logistics

In nearly all cases, the CPA must maintain an office at the employer brokerage firm's place of business. It is not necessary for the CPA to shutter an existing office that houses his practice, but he cannot under any circumstances give investment advice, discuss, offer, sell, or maintain literature on securities at that office. Such an office is neither a branch office nor a satellite office of the brokerage firm.

Client Profile

An alliance with an employed RR might be best for a CPA who typically serves a small business owner client profile with variable life insurance needs for buy-sell, key-man, or deferred compensation programs. Furthermore, a significant small business owner base may not provide a deep pool of securities investors; most have their personal assets squarely in their business, leaving life insurance products in the driver's seat, in which case an RR (versus an RIA) would be the more appropriate avenue.

If the CPA intends to market variable annuities exclusively or primarily as tax-savings strategies, an RR arrangement is sufficient from an immediate compensation perspective. The sophistication level of the CPA's clients will also help dictate which alliance to establish. Educated clients who exhibit a refined understanding of investing show more disdain toward commissioned products. They recognize the potential for an RR to lose objectivity when a product sale is involved.

> INVESTMENT ADVISER'S COMMENT
> *More than with any other investment product, there is a dramatic difference between what RRs receive in compensation from selling variable annuities and what RIAs receive. Commissionable variable annuities often pay in excess of 6 percent of the amount invested in the contract; on a $250,000 contract, that's $15,000 of commission. So if the variable annuity is a prime strategic means of accomplishing client goals, the RR structure (and compensation) is probably more attractive in the short term than an RIA's structure.*

Current Entity Size

A solo practitioner CPA more easily fits into any one of the RR selections than does a CPA firm with two or more CPAs. Singularity is the key. The decision-making energy of a one-person shop resides in a single brain and is filtered through a single set of opinions and principles. Once the decision hits, the licensing and all the paperwork involve a single person and it's a done deal. The solo CPA who believes that a high-visibility brokerage name impresses clients and is a powerful marketing tool is a perfect candidate for an alliance with an ERR.

If the CPA firm has more than one CPA as a decision maker, the likelihood of choosing an alliance with an ERR diminishes dramatically. Because a strategic alliance with an ERR imposes significant limitations on the individuals involved, the chances of getting two or more CPAs to agree to them and engage in the alliance could be described as slim to none.

Current Entity Business Structure

This is relevant only in that a business entity cannot become licensed as an RR. The CPA firm itself can be structured in any fashion. The strategic alliance is structured person-to-person: the CPA becomes an ERR licensed with the existing ERR.

Shared-Compensation Flow Inside the CPA Firm

There can be no direct or indirect sharing of the commissions (strategic alliance or otherwise) received by the licensed CPA with individuals within the CPA firm unless those persons are also licensed and affiliated with the same brokerage firm as the original CPA. It does not matter that the partner CPAs are located in a different office than the alliance CPA's office, which is maintained at the brokerage firm's offices.

Internal Marketing

Persuading key personnel inside the CPA firm to refer their clients to the licensed CPA of the alliance is a futile task at best. None of these personnel are likely to be licensed and are therefore unable to receive compensation for such referrals. So the impetus for sending clients to their fellow CPA is negligible.

Managing Clients' Perceptions

The CPA who enters an alliance with an ERR does so almost exclusively to benefit from the brokerage firm's recognized name in the market. As we've discussed, most other elements of this type of alliance are unfavorable. So the very decision to enter this alliance signals recognition that there is a single focus in managing client perceptions. The message to clients: "Look who I'm aligned with!"

INVESTMENT ADVISER'S COMMENT

Be careful with this; if your clients have had poor personal experiences with a particular brokerage firm, this philosophy can work against you. One other caveat: reputations of firms can rise and fall. One need only recall how quickly scandals have sullied the names of once-venerable brokerage houses.

Marketing to Clients

The most important initial factor the CPA must understand in marketing to his or her clients in this alliance is not what is said or what material is handed to the client, but from what location the action is performed. It cannot be from the office housing the CPA's practice. All investment documentation and communication must originate and conclude within the confines of the brokerage's official location. This includes mailing and phone campaigns, or any other direct client contact activity. This confinement forces the issue of marketing to clients back into the name recognition category. After all, if all paperwork meetings must occur in the brokerage firm's primary offices, all other elements of marketing become inconsequential. In summary, the CPA is on a very tight leash.

INVESTMENT ADVISER'S COMMENT

This is where our strategic alliance kicks in. If you get an investment inquiry from a client while sitting in your CPA office, tell the inquirer that your alliance partner will make contact forthwith. Then you call me with the contact info and I go to work. I'll keep you informed of the progress and if you want to connect to the case development at any time, you're more than welcome.

CPAs as "Client Advocate"

The ERR uses an array of products to complete the goals of clients. These products have varying commission payouts, which means if the RR recommends one over another, his commission is affected.

NASD rules and regulations attempt to force the RR to remain objective at all times. But in reality, this does not always occur. The RR's natural instinct of "me first" is an often-irresistible force that pulls him (and therefore his clients) toward products with larger commission payouts. To realize just how pervasive and influential this lure is, the RR need look no further than the size of the brokerage firm's compliance department and the constant scrutiny of its trading surveillance teams. These are in place to try to ensure the ERRs remain objective.

The CPA receives the same commission on the sale of products as the RR. However, unlike the ERR of this alliance, the CPA enjoys a separate flow of income, that of his accounting practice. So under normal conditions, the self-interest attraction is not as forceful.

Evolutionary Prognosis

The only dab of glue binding this alliance is the importance the CPA places on the brokerage firm's name recognition. The unique professional advantages the existing ERR in the alliance offers at the outset—knowledge and experience—will slowly dissolve with time. The CPA will strengthen in these areas. Because of this, and because the net commission left over after the brokerage cut is so meager, the sharing of compensation is likely to become a matter of dispute. The CPA will gravitate toward executing sales independently of the aligned ERR. The CPA is legally capable of doing this, employing his own brokerage-assigned identification number instead of the alliance group number, but still conducting business from the brokerage office only. By doing this, the CPA routes 100 percent of the commission to himself. This behavior will bring no chastisement from the brokerage firm. It will not pass judgment on the CPA's streak of autonomy. It does not care. To the firm business is business; it is irrelevant through which RR identification number that business flows.

If Needed, an Honorable Dissolution

Because of the severe rules and restrictions inherent in the operation of a larger brokerage firm, and the paltry net commissions the CPA will receive, this alliance will move very rapidly toward termination.

Nothing contractually binds the alliance, and therefore for perfectly good business reasons the CPA will ultimately break off revenue-sharing arrangements with the original RR and submit client sales applications under his own unique brokerage RR ID number.

Becoming a Registered Rep With an Existing Independent Registered Rep (IRR)

Regulatory/Licensing Requirements

The requirements are the same as those for becoming a registered rep with an existing employer registered rep (outlined above), except the CPA affiliates with the IRR's independent brokerage firm. The CPA must become a member of the NASD and pass the Series 6 test or the Series 7 test.

> INVESTMENT ADVISER'S COMMENT
>
> *Unlike an alliance with my colleague the ERR, you will be much less inclined to become a "do-it-yourselfer" after you run through licensing and become an IRR affiliated with my brokerage firm. This is not to imply that you are less entrepreneurial or intelligent than your CPA colleague aligning himself with the ERR. It is rather a recognition that the complex and thorough investment practice infrastructure in place and functioning in my practice would be daunting to duplicate. This infrastructure includes staffing, operations, equipment, lease arrangements, integrated compliance procedures, software, et cetera, none of which our alliance brokerage firm provides or pays for.*

Method of Compensation

Compensation is the same as when you become a registered rep with an existing employer registered rep, except the alliance receives an industry average payout from the brokerage firm of 85 percent, not 45 percent. As with the ERR alliance, the CPA and IRR each receive a unique personal identification number and together receive a unique group identification number from the brokerage firm, which allows them to receive commission on all joint sales.

INVESTMENT ADVISER'S COMMENT

The brokerage firm used by an independent RR has very little, if any, name recognition to the public. But this is precisely what an IRR wants. Most IRRs will tell you one of the reasons they are independent is because they don't want an aura of corporate affiliation. They contend the client/ adviser relationship is very personal and should not have to be subsidized by corporate image.

If you agree with this premise, then aligning with an IRR has greater objective value. At an 85 percent payout, it also has greater economic value. Unlike the situation with my ERR colleague, the 85 percent remains constant. There is no increase based on volume of production. Using his example, right up front we forfeit to the house (our independent brokerage firm) about 15 percent. So if we sell $50,000 of Class A mutual fund shares with a 5 percent front load, our alliance gets 85 percent of that, or $2,125. If our alliance split is fifty-fifty, we each get $1,062.50, or $437.50 more than a CPA/ERR alliance. This is a 70 percent increase in revenue. I will agree with my ERR friend that most of the work in landing the sale will come from the experience and operations capability of my practice, so I would concur that a seventy-thirty split is appropriate, unless of course the CPA burrows much more deeply into maintaining the relationship.

Potential Compensation Amount

Moderate.

Compliance

Same as when you become a registered rep with an existing employer registered rep, except when a CPA's office becomes a satellite to the IRR's branch office, something covered later in this chapter, the branch IRR must pay an annual visit to the CPA's office to audit all books and activity logs. The CPA abides by all the rules and regulations of the brokerage firm's best practices manual and the NASD. The same continuing education courses are required by the NASD or the brokerage firm.

INVESTMENT ADVISER'S COMMENT
Compliance oversight is accomplished by the process and procedures at work in our offices by our staff, as alluded to above. The cost of this responsibility is absorbed by my practice, not by the independent brokerage firm. I'm ultimately responsible for your behavior and actions in the investment market. If your license comes under fire, so does mine.

Office Logistics

The IRR maintains an office independent of the brokerage firm. The CPA in an alliance with an IRR can only conduct securities business from his primary office if that office becomes a registered satellite to the IRR's branch office. For compliance purposes, this tethers the CPA's office to the IRR's office, which is, in turn, tied to the brokerage firm's home office. In addition, the CPA must also place a notification in clear view in the office lobby stating that the office (and at least one individual in it) is affiliated with the specific IRR brokerage firm.

If the CPA's office does not become a registered satellite of the IRR's branch office, the CPA cannot conduct securities business from that office and he must maintain a communications presence (voice mail, e-mail, etc.) at the IRR's branch office.

Client Profile

Again, this element is identical to when you become a registered rep with an existing employer registered rep. Suitable CPA profiles would include: a heavy small business owner client profile with variable life insurance goals and clients in need of tax-deferral products, such as variable annuities. At the same time, a significant small business owner base may spell trouble for equities sales as this group normally invests much of what they have in their business. The more investment savvy the client base is, the less likely it is to accept commission as a means of compensation.

Current Entity Size

A sole proprietor practice is still an ideal candidate for this type of alliance. But with an IRR, so is the multi-CPA practice. A group of CPAs considering an arrangement with an IRR won't have to deal with the same prospective disadvantages as they would when contemplating an alliance with an ERR: low compensation and a dictated office location. The IRR has no such restrictions. Therefore, they're more likely to agree to the alliance. In fact, the very business model of the independent brokerage firm promotes the structure of branch offices and satellite offices.

INVESTMENT ADVISER'S COMMENT

A word of caution. If you're approached by an IRR who makes the claim of being a partner of a "group," such as the Midtown Investment Advisers Group, understand what you are really being told. A "group" of IRRs housed in the same office space may be doing so to share and therefore shrink the expense of operating each of their practices. Be assured, each IRR partner maintains his own private list of clients and rarely shares revenue with his fellow partners. Aside from a reduction in expenses, these arrangements are established to give the impression to each of the IRR's clients and prospects (including a potential alliance CPA) that they are engaging in a time-honored, cohesive entity that collectively looks after the welfare of all its IRR clients. This promotes a nice warm fuzzy feeling, which could be false. Although these arrangements may leave an erroneous impression, they're not illegal.

Current Entity Business Structure

As is the case when becoming a registered rep with an existing employer registered rep, a business entity cannot become an RR.

Shared-Compensation Flow Inside the CPA Firm

Compensation flow is the same as when becoming a registered rep with an existing employer registered rep. An RR cannot share commission with a business entity or with another person unless that person is also licensed and affiliated with the same brokerage firm as the RR.

Internal Marketing

The process of marketing such an alliance within a CPA firm is the same as it is for CPAs who become registered reps with an existing employer registered rep firm. Other personnel in the CPA firm who are not licensed cannot receive commission, which diminishes the chances of the strong referral flow to the licensed CPA of the firm.

Managing Clients' Perceptions

Unlike the CPA-ERR arrangement, an alliance with an IRR doesn't bring with it brokerage firm name recognition. The IRR alliance members counter this perceived disability by turning the tables and informing the CPA's clients that independence, not a prestigious name, is important to a serious relationship. Independence works in the client's favor because the alliance members aren't coerced to force-feed an employer's proprietary products into the recommendations mix. Nor is the independent RR under the pressure of meeting monthly life insurance sales goals set for him by his employer brokerage firm, which, in this case, would also be a life insurance company.

Marketing to Clients

Making the CPA's prime office a satellite of the IRR's branch office sweeps away any limits on where investment advice and activity can originate. The CPA is a licensed IRR operating in a legitimate compliance-managed location, with all the necessary regulatory ties to the independent brokerage.

This is essential in fulfilling the management of the clients' perception of independent investment advice outlined above. Having the ability to start and complete all documentation processes at the CPA office solidifies the notion of independence. This empowers the CPA to take command of any and all client marketing campaigns, which can originate from his primary office. Such control retains privacy over the CPA's client roster; he does not have to turn it over to an employer brokerage firm marketing department for addressing and mailing. The CPA can accept responses and inquiries at his practice office and not have to rely on voice mail at the brokerage firm location.

There are two methods of informing the CPA's clients about the new alliance: en masse and personal. The first usually leads to the second. With the en masse method, the CPA mails notifications (letters, marketing material, etc.) to clients announcing the strategic alliance and suggesting that if there is a need for investment advice, the trusted CPA firm is now open for business.

> **INVESTMENT ADVISER'S COMMENT**
> *Remember, though, the content of all your marketing communications, written for mail or handout or scripted for phone delivery, must be approved by me, your alliance partner and the branch manager IRR.*

CPAs as "Client Advocate"

Client advocacy remains the same as when becoming a registered rep with an existing employer registered rep. The sale of products with different payout structures potentially degrades an IRR's objectivity because one product recommendation will pay more commission than another.

Evolutionary Prognosis

Of all the RR alliance choices, this is the most lucrative and has the potential to endure the longest. The probability that the CPA will gradually pull away from the original IRR of the alliance and conduct business on his own is reduced by the structural flow of commission. In the ERR alliance, the CPA is tethered to the brokerage firm itself, which means commission moves directly from the brokerage to the CPA. In the IRR alliance, the CPA, as a satellite office, is threaded through the IRR's branch office for compliance control purposes, which means the CPA's commission stream flows through and is owned by the IRR and his branch office. So, on any individual investment activity outside the parameters of the alliance and executed out of the CPA's office, the IRR's branch office receives a "haircut," or a specific percent shaved off the 85 percent, agreed upon at the time the CPA becomes a satellite.

Here's an example of how $5,000 of commission would flow within an alliance whose split is seventy-thirty: brokerage sends $4,250 (85 percent) to the IRR's branch office; the IRR keeps $2,975 (70 percent) of that and sends $1,275 (30 percent) to the CPA's satellite office.

Here's an example of a $5,000 commission flow of CPA-only activity through the IRR branch with an agreed industry average "haircut" of 10 percent on nonalliance business: brokerage sends $4,250 (85 percent) to the IRR's branch office; the IRR keeps $425 (10 percent) and sends the balance of $3,825 to the CPA's satellite office. The CPA certainly enjoys a nice raise when acting outside the alliance, but the IRR is never left empty-handed. In fact, some branch manager IRRs will tell you they prefer their satellite IRRs to operate unassisted because the IRR's workload diminishes considerably.

If Needed, an Honorable Dissolution

If the alliance moves into rocky territory for whatever reason, the CPA can request that his license be housed at another branch of the brokerage firm. The CPA's commission would then flow through the new branch, which might have a different haircut payout. Branch IRRs are free to negotiate any haircut with their satellites they deem necessary to meet overhead and produce an acceptable profit. Some branches run more efficiently than others and therefore can afford to take a smaller haircut. There is one potential roadblock a CPA faces if he wants to realign with another branch—most independent brokerage firms give the current branch IRR the right to refuse permission for a satellite to switch to another branch.

This does not trap the CPA, but it complicates his life. He can live with the tension, resolve it, or affiliate with a branch of a different independent brokerage firm (or he can actually affiliate with an employer brokerage firm, as unwise as that might be). In some cases, if the CPA has a high production level, an independent brokerage firm will welcome his primary CPA office as an IRR branch itself. This, however, requires that the CPA pass the Series 24 test, which grants supervisory, branch manager status.

In reality, all these time-consuming and cumbersome procedures normally tend to serve as obstacles to actually dissolving an alliance.

> INVESTMENT ADVISER'S COMMENT
> *A couple of observations: 1) If a CPA/IRR changes independent broker-age firms, the paperwork can be excruciating. The CPA must get new, signed application documentation from every client who wants to follow him to his new home and 2) the Series 24 test is a fraction of an inch short of being as painful as the browbeating Series 7 test.*

Leasing Office Space to an Independent Registered Rep

Regulatory/Licensing Requirements

None.

Method of Compensation

Compensation comes from rental income from a lease arrangement with an IRR for office space and ancillary business services inside the CPA's office. The terms of this lease agreement must demonstrate arm's length clauses, reflect real estate market norms, and show no correlation to the IRR's commission.

> INVESTMENT ADVISER'S COMMENT
> *For at least the first year, I'm going to feel far more comfortable in a month-to-month arrangement in order to assess the long-term value of our alliance, especially if I'm maintaining a primary office elsewhere.*

Potential Compensation Amount

Very low.

Compliance

None, except it is wise for the CPA to possess the knowledge that the IRR cannot link rent payments to commissions produced by referrals sent to him. If the CPA agrees to some direct or indirect connection between the two, he must be aware that the IRR is violating NASD rules. Such a transgression would unlikely bring legal problems to the CPA, unless the origin of the discovery of the problem is the result of arbitration brought against the IRR by a disgruntled client; the CPA might have a difficult time claiming ignorance.

Office Logistics

There is no change, other than grappling with the nuances of a tenant-landlord relationship.

Client Profile

Promising prospective clients would include all those who must file a tax return and who have sufficient assets to consider investments, including adults and business owners with life insurance needs.

Current Entity Size

To some degree, current entity size is irrelevant. However, the smaller the CPA firm, the more dominant the physical presence of the IRR to clients as they visit the CPA office. If not managed properly, this could be a negative factor. However, if marketed creatively, it could be a positive.

Current Entity Business Structure

The current entity business structure is irrelevant.

Shared-Compensation Flow Inside the CPA Firm

The rent payments go right to the CPA's profit & loss statement.

Internal Marketing

From the CPA's perspective, there is only a vague tie between the value of the services offered by the lessee IRR to the CPA's clients and incoming rent revenue. Because there is no direct correlation, the IRR gradually becomes nothing more than a tenant methodically funneling rent payments to the CPA.

INVESTMENT ADVISER'S COMMENT
If you take in an IRR possessing even a small dose of marketing skills, be advised he will not allow this complacency to settle in—or at least he shouldn't. An aggressive IRR will make certain the CPAs in the firm

know he is there, why he is there and, much more delicately, that a dry pipeline of referrals might necessitate voiding the monthly lease. If a CPA client needs investment advice from an IRR, there is no reason not to escort the client down the hall to the IRR's office. In this arrangement, that's the CPA's only task. The firm has fulfilled its obligation. The IRR's inability to close the sale is not the concern of the CPA firm.

Managing Clients' Perceptions

The importance of this and the next category ("Marketing to Clients") depends entirely on the CPA firm's depth of purpose. If, from the CPA firm's perspective, the IRR's presence is more a means of rent revenue and less a means of conveniently offering supplemental service to its clients, the alliance is shallow and won't flourish. In this circumstance, managing the perceptions of the CPA firm's clients is irrelevant. The firm's CPA partners simply won't care. The IRR is nothing more than a tenant.

However, if the CPA firm's purpose in the alliance is meaningful, then managing its clients' perception as to why there is an investment adviser in the CPA offices becomes imperative. The most accurate explanation is also the one that occupies the highest moral ground: the investment adviser is in the CPA offices as an added service to clients, and the CPA firm receives no monetary benefit if the client chooses to work with the investment adviser.

INVESTMENT ADVISER'S COMMENT

The CPA firm and the IRR might make this rent-only choice a first step toward an alliance where one of the CPAs becomes an IRR and shares in commission generated from the clients the CPA firm sends down the hall. If this is the case, the CPA needs to be careful about boasting that the firm receives no monetary benefit from the relationship. Eventually this statement will be false, and the CPAs will find themselves in the uncomfortable ethical position of having to verbally reverse this declaration to clients.

Marketing to Clients

Because a fixed rent is the means of CPA revenue, the firm has no incentive to extend marketing efforts beyond merely introducing clients to the IRR at the time of office visits and when a client expresses an interest in investments.

> **INVESTMENT ADVISER'S COMMENT**
> *On the other hand, if this is the first step to a licensed IRR alliance as mentioned above, the CPA firm might want to launch a more assertive marketing campaign as a means of testing the degree of client interest and potential for commissions. If the client response is substantial, the CPA firm might consider moving immediately from the rent alliance to the licensed IRR alliance, where commissions generated from the clients' positive reaction can be realized.*

CPAs as "Client Advocate"

Because the CPA's revenue in this alliance has no connection to the IRR's commission, the CPA sits squarely with the client opposite the IRR. The CPA is in a position to ask the IRR tough questions on behalf of the client about the recommendations being offered.

Evolutionary Prognosis

This relationship will encounter three possible degrees of success: sturdy, grudging, and frail. 1) A sturdy success is one in which the CPA firm consciously refers as many clients as it deems in need, and the IRR responds with diligence and professionalism. 2) A grudging success is one in which the IRR has to continuously squeeze referrals from the CPA firm. 3) A frail success is one in which one of the two alliance members ceases to perform to the expectation of the other member.

More times than not, this alliance choice commences at the sturdy stage, slides to grudging, and dissolves after frailty. To check this degradation, each party should recognize its possibility and work to prevent it.

If Needed, an Honorable Dissolution

The decision to dissolve this alliance lies almost entirely with the IRR. If the IRR cannot quantifiably justify the alliance—meaning income from the CPA referrals is less than the rent payments—it will end. At the outset of the alliance, a sense of hope and potential play a qualitative part in the IRR's overall analysis. Eventually, though, CPA referral track record will push the entire analysis onto the quantitative side of the ledger.

On the other hand, if the IRR is not performing his professional duties in the manner the CPA firm believes he should, the CPA firm isn't likely to terminate the lease; it will merely refer its clients elsewhere and continue to accept the IRR's rent check.

Providing Consulting to an Independent Registered Rep

Regulatory/Licensing Requirements

None.

Method of Compensation

The CPA firm charges the IRR for advice and consultation on tax and related topics on behalf of the clients the CPA firm refers to the IRR. This can be done using an hourly rate or a retainer. As with the leasing alliance, the invoiced amount can have no correlation to the amount of commission generated by the sale of products to the referred clients. In fact, if a regulatory body audits the IRR and it is discovered that the CPA invoiced only on referrals that became IRR clients, the auditors will more than likely cite this as evidence of correlation between monies paid and commissions.

> INVESTMENT ADVISER'S COMMENT
> *The only time I'd be comfortable with a retainer fee instead of an hourly charge is after years of a successful alliance.*

Potential Compensation Amount

Low.

Compliance

The compliance process is the same as with an arrangement that leases office space to an IRR.

Office Logistics

Most of the time, the CPA firm referral will prefer to conduct the first few initial meetings with the IRR at the CPA offices. It is these meetings that are the basis for invoiced time by the CPA.

> INVESTMENT ADVISER'S COMMENT
>
> *I also prefer meetings be held at the CPA's offices. Familiar surroundings and the presence of the CPA during the first few meetings inject a huge dose of credibility to my practice.*
>
> *There's an element of this alliance that IRRs will feel uncomfortable with: "out of sight, out of mind." If the IRR comes face-to-face with the CPAs in the firm only on occasion, the CPAs are not constantly reminded that the IRR's service is available to their clients and they let prospects slip away without realizing it. On the flip side, because the IRR does not see the CPAs regularly, the IRR loses the opportunity to battle the effects of the aforementioned cliché.*

Client Profile

The client profile would be the same as when a CPA firm leases office space to an IRR.

Current Entity Size

In most cases, the smaller the CPA firm, the better. The key factor dictating the success of this alliance is revenue impact on the CPA firm's profit. A sole proprietor CPA will notice revenue more readily than a large firm and will want it to continue. The exception to this is if each partner of a large CPA firm makes an earnest commitment to refer and the firm makes a concerted effort to track and report to its partners the revenue generated as a result of the activity. This converts each partner of the large firm into the same mental state as the sole proprietor.

Current Entity Business Structure

This factor is irrelevant in this arrangement.

Shared-Compensation Flow Inside the CPA Firm

The invoice payments go to the CPA's profit & loss statement.

Internal Marketing

Unlike the lease alliance, there is a direct link between a referral and an invoice. As stated, however, there cannot be a direct correlation between the commission from the referral and the amount of the invoice. Because hourly fees and the invoicing process are already part of the CPA firm's culture, CPA firms find this type of alliance more suitable and this helps encourage the firm's members to refer.

Managing Clients' Perceptions

Because the IRR is not housed in the CPA offices, taking the position that the CPAs are offering an added service for their clients is less tenable than if the IRR maintained a physical presence. From the client's perspective, because the IRR is off-site and the CPA firm bills the IRR for consultation, the alliance replicates more of a standard business arrangement than something distinctive. This diminishes the need to frame the alliance in a special manner.

Marketing to Clients

The client perceptions outlined above might preclude a vigorous marketing campaign. The alternative is to refer as needed. However, the CPA firm could introduce the alliance to its clients by inviting them to meet the IRR in a seminar or workshop setting at the CPA offices.

CPAs as "Client Advocate"

As with leasing office space to an IRR, the CPA maintains objectivity because there is no relationship between the IRR's commission and the amount the CPA will invoice the IRR for advice rendered.

Evolutionary Prognosis

Unlike the lease alliance, the strength of this alliance does not depend on the depth of purpose of the CPAs. The strength depends on the accumulation of a single act: sending referrals to the IRR. Without referrals, there is no invoicing and thus no revenue. The faucet is either off or on. The hand on the faucet belongs solely to the CPA firm and how wide it opens the spigot determines the success of the alliance. If revenue from invoicing the IRR becomes noticeable over time, the more turns the faucet will get.

There are two circumstances under which the flow would eventually cease: the impact of the revenue generated is inconspicuous and/or the IRR is negligent. If commitment among the CPA partners is sporadic and there are no internal means of keeping the invoice revenues front and center, the CPA firm is less likely to notice the profit and the alliance will fade in significance. If the IRR is not diligent in his relationship with the referrals sent to him (late to meetings, poor follow-up, not keeping his word, etc.), the message will eventually migrate back to the CPAs, who will undoubtedly terminate the alliance.

What is not a valid circumstance is the IRR's weakness in closing the sale of product. Invoicing cannot occur exclusively on those referrals that generated commissions. If the CPAs and IRR maintain this rule, and the IRR yields low closing rates, the IRR will experience continuous losses as a result of paying invoices on referrals the IRR could not convert to clients.

If Needed, an Honorable Dissolution

Dissolving the alliance is quite simple. The CPA firm informs the IRR that it intends to stop referring clients, or the IRR, suffering losses, stops accepting referrals. Alliance dissolved.

Combination of the Previous Four

There are a multitude of variations on the above four RR alliances; to attempt a point-by-point analysis of each is beyond the scope of this book. A few factors are regulatory-driven and constant throughout any variation: method of compensation, licensing, compliance, and shared-compensation flow inside the CPA firm.

As well, an individual cannot be an employed RR and an independent RR at the same time. An RR cannot be affiliated with more than one brokerage firm simultaneously.

Next up, the many facets of an RIA/CPA alliance are reviewed.

7 | CPAs and Registered Investment Advisers (RIAs)

A registered investment adviser (RIA) is an entirely different creature from a registered rep (RR). The difference is highlighted in the section called "Ownership and Structure," which adds fourteen subfactors to our list of factors to bear in mind when CPAs are considering an alliance with an RIA. Before we examine these new elements, let's summarize the RIA. First we'll review the RIA profile.

Types of Registered Investment Advisers

1 Brokerage-based—owned and controlled by a national or regional independent or employer brokerage firm, established to allow the firm's employed RRs to offer fee-based advice.

2 Autonomous associated—owned and controlled by an independent RR or a group of independent RRs so they can offer fee-based advice to clients without using their affiliated brokerage-based RIA.

3 Autonomous unassociated—owned and controlled by a person or a group who is not a member of the NASD and not affiliated with a brokerage firm.

Registered Investment Adviser Alliance Choices

1 The CPA is a solicitor for an RIA
2 The CPA is an investment adviser (IA) registered with an RIA
3 The CPA is a passive (noncontrolling) owner of an RIA
4 The CPA is an active (controlling) owner of an RIA

Moving from one to four, the choices become more private and potentially more lucrative.

For each of these choices the following factors are examined that will assist the CPA in formulating a decision about which choice best fits which entity. The "Ownership and Structure" section reflects how differently the RIA is constructed, regulated, and presented to the market as compared with the RR. The RIA is a business entity with ownership and business structure issues; the RR must be a human being.

The CPA firm should expect the RIA to have established some definitive parameters for the subfactors in the Ownership and Structure category. This is not to imply that many of the items won't end up on the negotiating table. Some satisfy various regulatory demands and aren't flexible. In the explanations below, an entry of "nonnegotiable" will accompany a factor that is inflexible.

1 Ownership and Structure

There are three elements of ownership: client assets under management, the fee-based revenue stream produced by those assets, and who within the alliance owns how much of that revenue stream.

A common misconception in valuing an RIA practice and/or an alliance with an RIA is that the RIA is in control of the client assets that throw off the fee-based revenue stream. This is folly. The clients themselves own the assets. Ownership is ultimate control, wielded only by the client. The RIA is at the mercy of this control, which means the client can move the assets elsewhere for management, thus ending the revenue stream to the RIA.

From a traditional perspective, the RIA owns the revenue stream of the client assets. But even this assertion is tenuous. After all, if the clients own the assets, then they indirectly own the revenue stream; if they control the assets, then they control the revenue stream of the assets. What the RIA really owns are the "current rights" to the relationship with its clients. The RIA uses the revenue streams of its clients to translate these current rights into quantifiable value on its balance sheet.

In light of this perspective, it is quite easy to understand how powerful the common declaration "It's the relationship that counts" is in the financial profession. The client relationship is the real value of ownership.

These are the questions that must be answered by the CPAs and the RIA in discussing a strategic alliance:

a Ownership of revenue stream—does the CPA firm own the first rights to the revenue stream of those clients it referred to the RIA and how is that asset base valued? What occurs if the RIA is bought?

b Capital contribution—does the RIA require the CPA firm to commit a lump sum of money to engage in the alliance?

c Shares owned—are the RIA firm's shares issued to the CPA, and if so, what class of shares?

d Revenue-sharing rate—what percentage of the assets under management fee does the CPA firm receive for referrals sent to the RIA?

e RIA financial disclosure—is it justifiable for the CPA firm to request information on the RIA firm's financial health?

f Noncompete agreement—under what, if any, circumstances can the CPA compete with the RIA if the agreement terminates?

g RIA employee (nonnegotiable)—what is the tax status of the CPA?

h Voting rights (nonnegotiable)—under what conditions does the CPA have voting rights?

i Legalities—what legal documents must be generated to formalize the alliance?

j Tax reporting (nonnegotiable)—how is the CPA's income reported to the IRS?

k RIA approval—what procedures within the RIA are followed to approve of the alliance?

l Retirement trigger—under what circumstances does the CPA voluntarily cease participation in the alliance?

m Retirement payout period—for how long does the CPA continue to receive shared revenue of referrals on the RIA's books?

n Retirement buyout—what happens to the shared revenues if the RIA is bought after the CPA enters the retirement phase?

o Retirement example summary—a quantitative snapshot of the impact of l, m, and n.

2 Regulatory/licensing requirements—what is required of the CPA firm by law to engage in this alliance?

3 Method of compensation—How is the CPA firm compensated, and is this element negotiable?

4 Potential compensation amount—how much compensation can the CPA expect, relative to all other alliance choices?

5 Compliance—what daily compliance issues, if any, does the CPA firm face and at roughly what cost?

6 Office logistics—Where must the CPA firm be located to legally do business?

7 Client profile—How well does a CPA's existing client base match the RIA's existing client base?

8 Current entity size—does the size of the CPA firm in any way affect which choice of strategic alliance structure is most suitable?

9 Current entity business structure—Similarly, does the CPA firm's current business structure affect which alliance choice is best?

10 Shared-compensation flow inside the CPA firm—what happens with the alliance revenue once it gets inside the CPA firm?

11 Internal marketing among CPA partners, managers, and others—what are the best methods for rallying the troops around the alliance?

12 Managing clients' perceptions of the alliance—what is the best way to present the new alliance to the CPA's client base?

13 Marketing to clients (current and future)—what marketing techniques work best?

14 CPAs as the "Client Advocate"—Can the CPA, who is sharing in some capacity the revenue generated by the client's engagement of the RIA, ethically and honestly maintain objectivity? There is a solid argument that, in varying degrees, the CPA can be impartial in an RIA alliance, especially relative to the degree of objectivity attained in an RR alliance. A CPA/RIA alliance delivers a fee-based service to the CPA's clients. This puts the CPA firm in a better position than in an alliance with an RR to assert that it has the best interest of the client at heart and will dutifully monitor the tax implications of the RIA's investment activity. Each of the four RIA alliance choices presents slight variations from different perspectives.

15 Evolutionary prognosis—what might each strategic alliance type look like in the future and why will it take its shape?

16 If needed, an honorable dissolution—how to escape cleanly and honorably from the alliance.

As with the RR, many of these factors repeat themselves throughout the four RIA alliance choices. When they do repeat themselves, their occurrence in other organizational structures is indicated and their significance is summarized. Some are irrelevant and are noted as such.

Solicitor's Agreement With an RIA

Ownership and Structure

Ownership of Revenue Stream
No.

Capital Contribution
None.

Shares Owned
None issued.

Revenue-Sharing Rate
A good benchmark is the rate Schwab Institutional requires from

RIAs to which it sends referrals: 15 percent of the RIA's fee. However, in order to incentivize prolonged activity and to gauge how serious the CPA firm is, the RIA might present a two- or three-tiered scale, perhaps starting at 10 percent up to a certain level of referral assets managed, moving to 12.5 percent for a second level, and finally settling at 15 percent for assets over a final level.

From the RIA's perspective the ultimate percentage is a product of how much effort, time, and professional noninvestment expertise it thinks the CPA will supply to the client relationship. Both parties must decide what part of this assistance contributes to the client's happiness.

The base of the solicitor percentage is the total asset management fee collected from the client's account. This total fee is a product of the RIA's asset management percentage scale. This is important to understand because the higher the RIA management fee, the greater absolute dollar revenue the CPA firm may realize. On the other hand, the greater the fees, relative to what other RIAs are asking, the greater the potential for lost assets.

> **Investment Adviser's Comment**
>
> *You might think 10 percent to 15 percent of a 1 percent asset management fee seems awfully meager compared to 25 percent of 85 percent commission on mutual fund shares. But remember, asset management fees hit your wallet every quarter. All things being equal, with annual fees you'll break even relative to commission in slightly more than four years and you will have doubled your money in nine years. But you have to keep the fee-based client happy, which is what makes fee-based work a service while commission-based work is a product sale.*

RIA Financial Disclosure

The RIA can choose to share its financial data (P&L, balance sheet, etc.) with a CPA prior to engaging in the alliance. However the RIA firm might conclude that its desire to keep this information private outweighs the CPA's need to know, at least with the solicitor choice of an alliance structure.

Noncompete Agreement

This should be addressed in the solicitor's agreement or as a stand-alone document. Expect the RIA to introduce this to the CPA firm. If the CPA firm is not constrained by a noncompete clause or document, the RIA could suffer the loss of clients if the CPA firm dissolves the alliance, reemerges in an alliance with a competitor RIA, and begins siphoning off clients it had referred to the original RIA. A noncompete document should prohibit this or similar behavior.

> ### INVESTMENT ADVISER'S COMMENT
> *Of the four RIA alliance choices, as a solicitor you're the least likely to break away and compete against the RIA. The barriers to market entry—specifically licensing and office infrastructure—are higher for you than those of the other three alliance types.*

RIA Employee

No. A clause within the solicitor's agreement should indicate that the relationship between the RIA and the CPA is not that of employer and employee. The CPA firm is an independent contractor.

Voting Rights

None.

Legalities

Solicitor's agreement, disclosure statement, noncompete document.

Tax Reporting

Form 1099.

RIA Approval

This is an internal matter; however, it would seem reasonable that a majority of the partners of the RIA firm should agree to engage a CPA in a solicitor's agreement.

Retirement Trigger

The reason for any of these alliances to exist is to generate and share revenue on clients referred by the CPA firm to the RIA. So if the CPA firm stops or drastically reduces the referral activity, the sole basis for the alliance deteriorates. The potential for this is much less likely in a large CPA firm, where continuity of business is paramount. But a sole proprietor might retire and head to Florida.

> INVESTMENT ADVISER'S COMMENT
> *You can expect the RIA to place a time restriction requiring a specific number of qualified referred clients. For example: if your firm does not send at least one qualified referral per quarter, the RIA has the right to move your firm into the retirement phase. You might ask for the right to appeal such a ruling, since it may have temporarily lost its focus on the alliance.*

Retirement Payout Period

Since entering the retirement phase of the alliance is not the same as terminating it, the retired CPA firm can expect to continue receiving its shared revenue for a period of time. This can be arbitrary and is negotiable.

A quantitative method might have the retiring CPA continuing to receive shared revenue on its referred clients' assets for x number of months for every x number of months the alliance existed. For example: for every twelve months the CPA firm remains in the solicitor alliance, it receives two months of continued shared revenue upon retirement. In this example, if the CPA firm is a solicitor for five years and retires, it receives ten months of continued shared revenue. These two variables can be arrived at by an analysis of expected return on investment (past and future) if the RIA wants to delve into this deeply.

> INVESTMENT ADVISER'S COMMENT
> *The CPA should know that some solicitor's agreements have no Retirement Payout Period. Many RIAs believe that when you discontinue sending referrals the RIA's way under the specific circumstances outlined in the agreement, the solicitor's agreement itself is null and void and all future revenue ceases.*

Retirement Buyout

As a solicitor, the CPA has no ownership claim to the revenue stream from the clients it referred.

Retirement Example Summary

A CPA firm that has been a solicitor for five years at 15 percent of fees, or $22,500 annually ($150,000 times 15 percent), receives ten months (at two months for every twelve months in the alliance) of continued shared revenue after entering the retirement phase. The sum after ten months equals $18,750.

Regulatory/Licensing Requirements

Some states do not require a solicitor to become licensed by passing the NASD's Series 65 test, but most do. In these states, if the CPA firm is a business entity other than a sole proprietorship, one person in the firm, preferably a partner, must pass the Series 65 test and become the conduit through which referrals pass to the RIA and compensation is returned to the CPA firm.

Which states have requirements and which do not is difficult to track because those requirements change with time and with politics. All of the NASD Series tests require an individual to retain a sponsor. In the case of an RR, the sponsor is the retail brokerage firm with which the RR has affiliated. Because RIAs don't affiliate with retail brokerage firms, the sponsor usually becomes either the RIA or the RIA's state of domicile.

Method of Compensation

Fee-based. Unlike the solitary commission event on the sale of a product, fees are continuous. Most of the time they are based on assets under management and experience market growth, which means the fees can increase as the size of the account increases. The percentage fee the CPA receives from the RIA for referring clients is a matter of negotiation, as discussed above under "Revenue-Sharing Rate."

INVESTMENT ADVISER'S COMMENT
If the RIA is also affiliated with a broker-dealer—or is one itself—there is a very high probability that some compensation generated from referrals you send to the RIA will be commission and not fees. Set expectations with the understanding that these commissions can't be shared with you. In fact, on occasion revenue generated might be all commission, especially if the client only needs life insurance or annuities.

Potential Compensation Amount

Moderately high.

Compliance

The CPA firm and the RIA enter into a written solicitor's agreement outlining the details of the arrangement. This document is kept on file at the RIA's office; a copy does not have to be given to the client. What does have to be provided to and signed by the client is a Disclosure Statement, revealing six pieces of information about the solicitor's agreement: the solicitor's name, the RIA's name, the detailed nature of the relationship, that the solicitor will be paid by the RIA, how much and how often, and if the client's fees are higher than the RIA's normal fees as a result of the solicitor's agreement.

INVESTMENT ADVISER'S COMMENT
There are two areas of the solicitor's agreement you need to be keenly aware of: the personal integrity questions and marketing prohibitions. If you or your firm has been in any financial or legal (commercial and/or criminal) trouble in the past, you can't put your John Hancock on the agreement. If you pass this first test and become a solicitor, you can't talk about investments to referrals because you're not licensed to do so.

Yes, you do have strong opinions and some strong fundamental knowledge of investments, but you are not licensed so the SEC doesn't care what you think of your personal expertise.

Office Logistics

It is unnecessary for the RIA to portray the image of being an integral part of the CPA firm by maintaining an office within its confines. The CPA firm is usually the point of first contact between the referral and the RIA. Most subsequent meetings will be conducted at the RIA's offices.

Client Profile

The CPA's primary client profile should be nearly identical to the RIA's, which is heavily investment oriented and with fewer life insurance needs. The entire RIA model is built to provide investment advice and the management of investment assets. Fees for the management of sub-accounts in life insurance policies are not usually a potent profit center for an RIA.

The CPA holding a strong and nearly exclusive presence in the small business market, where much of an owner's assets are committed to the business itself, might not be a good candidate for an alliance with an RIA, unless the RIA itself seeks small business retirement programs.

Current Entity Size

This becomes significant once a decision is made about the next topic, Current Entity Business Structure. If the CPA firm itself becomes the solicitor, or creates a separate entity to accept the revenue stream from referrals, size is irrelevant. If each CPA within the firm becomes an individual solicitor, then the CPA firm size becomes important. The RIA's management of numerous alliance relationships can be awkward and ultimately nonproductive.

Current Entity Business Structure

A CPA firm, whether a one-person show or multipartnered, is organized as some form of business entity. The most effortless means of structuring the alliance is to make that entity the solicitor for the RIA. The creation of a separate business entity to act as the alliance solicitor makes sense for two reasons. The first is to help shield the CPA firm and the RIA firm from potential liability. The second is that certain partners may have no interest in participating in the alliance. In this case those partners and/or managers who will contribute would hold ownership in the new entity.

Of course, rather than creating a separate business entity, individual partners could choose to become solicitors. This method is more appropriate in small firms, particularly if not all the partners are interested in the alliance. The RIA establishes individual alliances with each partner or manager who is interested. The disadvantage to the CPAs acting as individual solicitors, as opposed to the firm being the solicitor, comes if the RIA has a multitiered payout structure. In that case, the firm would reach the tier levels much more rapidly than would each individual.

Shared-Compensation Flow Inside the CPA Firm

If the CPA firm, or a separately created entity, is the solicitor in the alliance, the firm itself receives the proceeds from the RIA. After the CPA firm receives the money, its further distribution is a nonregulatory issue.

Recall that some states require that an individual within a business entity that is a solicitor become licensed by passing the NASD's Series 65 test. In these cases, the shared revenues must flow from the RIA to that individual, who can then redistribute at will. (As CPAs well know, there are additional tax ramifications for this individual.)

Internal Marketing

The RIA has an obligation to contribute to the success of the alliance by educating all the CPA partners about the RIA's investment policies, practices, and procedures and then convincing the partners of the benefits for each of them and their clients. Initially this is best accomplished by gathering all the partners involved and giving a presentation on the proposed alliance. If not provided, the CPA firm should request from the RIA a pro forma demonstrating the potential profit for the solicitor, as this will help persuade the accountants of the benefits they stand to reap.

Managing Clients' Perceptions

A solicitor for an RIA is the least private of the four RIA choices. The referred client must sign a disclosure document that stipulates the pertinent facts of the solicitor's agreement between the RIA and the CPA firm. One of the data points is how much money, or what percentage of the management fee collected from the client, is passed on to the CPA.

Fortunately the CPA has ample justification for being in the fee loop. There is a direct connection between investment advice and strategy and tax planning, especially in cases involving estates. The CPA should remain engaged with the RIA on behalf of the client's investment tax matters. (This rationale is far more difficult to establish for professionals other than CPAs.)

Marketing to Clients

The CPA firm that forms a solicitor alliance with an RIA must decide right from the start how strong its commitment is to the alliance. The magnitude of that commitment will dictate the breadth of client marketing.

CPA firms that show more energy toward keeping the referral pipeline full will proudly display and present the alliance shoulder-to-shoulder with the CPA's practice itself. Investment advice as a parallel and equally important service will be part of marketing material, letterhead, and business cards. The CPA firm might host in-house investment seminars for its clients as a means of introducing them to the alliance.

The CPA firm with a casual commitment might, only after reviewing that client's tax return, provide the client with the name and phone number of the RIA, making little or no effort to arrange an introductory meeting.

CPAs as "Client Advocate"

The CPA firm cannot act as an advocate of the client by passing judgment on investment advice delivered by the RIA. Doing so would be the same as giving advice, which the solicitor is not licensed to do. However, the CPA firm can act as a client advocate on all other matters—fees, how often reviews occur, what reports should be provided, and so forth.

The CPA firm in a solicitor alliance with an RIA is detached from the RIA. It has no ownership interest in the RIA firm. The argument could be made that nonownership is the more appropriate position to maintain objectivity because the CPA firm has no interest in the revenue stream of the RIA, and that the only interest lies in the sharing of the asset management fees from each referred client. The analysis in the upcoming section on ownership RIAs will offer an opposing position.

Evolutionary Prognosis

The strength and endurance of a solicitor alliance depends on a number of factors, including the relationship between the CPA firm and the RIA before the alliance, the RIA's marketing ability, the real commitment of the CPA firm, the RIA's business practices, and the reporting and fee payment to the CPA.

If the principals of the CPA firm and those of the RIA already have a history of friendship and/or revenue-less referrals, a solicitor alliance would commence from a foundation of trust and fulfilled expectations and have a high probability of long-term success. If the two firms are newly introduced, that foundation is weak and untested. Strengthening the alliance's underpinning depends on two factors: CPA commitment and RIA business practices. The commitment of the CPA firm might be stable going into the alliance, but because of the newness of the relationship between the CPA firm and the RIA, it is, in fact, raw and untested. It could deteriorate rapidly.

The onus of preventing this lies squarely with the RIA. The RIA must perform a number of actions to convince the CPA firm the alliance is worthwhile and to infuse vigor into the relationship. It should relentlessly market the benefits of the alliance to the individual CPAs of the firm. When dealing with CPA referrals it is essential the RIA observe business practices of the highest order (be on time for meetings, perform thorough follow-up, keep his or her word, etc.). The RIA must also provide the CPA firm with consistent, accurate reporting on the status of its referrals, and pay the CPA firm its share of the fees, accompanied by documentation, on a regular schedule.

Executing these quality business practices will convince the CPA firm that its new alliance partner means business. Failing to follow these practices will result in weakness of the alliance.

If Needed, an Honorable Dissolution

There are two means of dissolving the solicitor alliance: the CPA firm enters the retirement phase (discussed earlier) or either party terminates the agreement. There are various reasons why either alliance member would want to terminate the agreement, but only a few are prominent. The CPA firm would most likely end the alliance if the RIA is incapable of performing its responsibilities outlined above. The RIA will—not might, but will—terminate the alliance if any individual within the CPA firm that is not licensed dispenses investment advice to the alliance clients. This is a violation of the solicitor's agreement itself and of the Investment Advisers Act of 1940.

If the alliance is terminated because the solicitor violates any rule, regulation, or part of the 1940 Act, the shared revenue stream should cease.

Investment Adviser (IA) With an RIA

Multipartner CPA firms will have little, if any, interest in this alliance choice. An IA registered with an RIA must be a human being, not a business entity. Certainly one of the individual CPA partners could become licensed and then register as an IA with the RIA. But, with one exception, the CPA firm could accomplish the same goals by merely entering into a solicitor alliance with the RIA.

The lone exception is the level of privacy the CPA who has registered as an IA sustains. As has been discussed, a solicitor of an RIA must require clients to sign a document that outlines certain parameters of the solicitor's agreement, including the amount of fees the CPA receives from the RIA. As an IA with an RIA, client disclosure occurs in the RIA's ADV Part II, which is provided to the client before engagement. This document provides, among hundreds of other data points about the RIA, information on the IA's education, employment background, and roughly how many hours a week the

IA devotes to being an IA. It does not specify how much of the client fee the IA receives.

Because an IA alliance is more practical for the sole-proprietor CPA, the following points will be analyzed as such.

Ownership and Structure

Ownership of Revenue Stream
No.

Capital Contribution
None.

Shares Owned
None issued.

Revenue-Sharing Rate
The CPA could rightfully contend that an IA alliance is more stable and more lucrative for the RIA because the CPA must become licensed. Doing so requires time and money, two solid indicators of commitment. As we see in the "Marketing to Clients" section, there are three service styles from which the CPA/IA operates—oversee, assist, advise. The amount of time and effort required by the CPA increases with each style. The oversee style requires more work of the CPA than that of a solicitor CPA who merely delivers a client. Perhaps its fee rate should start at 17.5 percent. The rate should move upward per service style, to perhaps 20 percent for the assist level and 22.5 percent for those clients in the advise stage.

> **INVESTMENT ADVISER'S COMMENT**
> *As a CPA/IA, it's best that you keep these three options open and fluid with incoming clients and work out a fee-sharing arrangement that's just as flexible. You might want to be an "overseer" with some clients, an "assistant" with some, and an actual "adviser" with others. The RIA should not care which style you employ as long as you hold the style steady throughout the relationship. You shouldn't bring a client in as an "adviser" and then deliver the time and service level of an "overseer." The RIA will call you on it.*

RIA Financial Disclosure

An RIA will be reluctant to share this data with an IA. Surely the CPA/IA might argue that knowledge of the RIA's financial solvency (or insolvency) is important if he is to refer clients. After all, the CPA's reputation is on the line, too, when he or she refers clients. But this is a weak stand because the CPA is licensed and if the RIA foundered, the IA could either become an IA for another RIA or become an RIA himself and move his clients. The solvency of an RIA has no direct effect on the account balances of clients, because an RIA doesn't have custody of client assets.

> INVESTMENT ADVISER'S COMMENT
>
> *If you want a general, quick snapshot of the volume of business the RIA has booked, ask to see the past three to five years of ADV Part II. Go to item number five, "Information About Your Advisory Business." This section discloses the number of an RIA's employees, clients, and assets under management. With a three- to five-year history you can detect growth or deterioration.*
>
> *Also, if you decide to deliver clients to the RIA as a full "adviser" and the RIA falters, you'll be in a better position from the clients' perspective to transition them to your own newly formed RIA or one with which you register because you will have been in much firmer control of the relationship and the client will regard you—not the sinking RIA—as the pivot.*

Noncompete Agreement

The CPA will be required to sign a noncompete agreement. As mentioned above, the IA is licensed and could depart the RIA alliance, establish a new one, and carry all previously referred clients with him, irrespective of the financial health of the original RIA. A noncompete agreement will prevent this. However, the IA should request a clause in the agreement that protects him from the condition outlined above; if the RIA wobbles financially, the IA is free to escape with all referred clients in hand.

RIA Employee

The only condition in which this might apply is if the CPA operates his practices from the RIA's offices. Based on the CPA's personal circumstances, becoming an employee of the RIA might be favorable (employee benefits, future partner potential, possible higher revenue-sharing rate, etc.). The alternative to employee status is independent contractor status.

> INVESTMENT ADVISER'S COMMENT
> *Both the RIA and the individual CPA need to assess this employee/ employer relationship. There are several crucial questions to consider. Will both the RIA and the CPA share its current client base? How much salary (and how is it calculated) does the CPA receive? Can the CPA add clients to his practice and not share subsequent revenue with the RIA? These and other questions, unique to the two parties, should be examined closely prior to the CPA becoming an employee.*

Voting Rights
None.

Legalities
Noncompete clause; employment agreement, if applicable.

Tax Reporting
Form 1099, as an independent contractor. Form W-2, as an employee.

RIA Approval
Majority vote of the active partners.

Retirement Trigger
Same as a solicitor alliance; the CPA agrees that if there are no referrals sent to the RIA over a specific period of time, the CPA retires from the IA position and the retirement payout period begins.

Retirement Payout Period
Same as a solicitor alliance, except the CPA/IA can contend that the payout period variables be more favorable than those of the CPA in

a solicitor alliance, employing the identical argument applied to the revenue-sharing rate of an immediate 15 percent. Instead of the solicitor's receipt of two months of continued revenue sharing for every twelve months in the alliance, the CPA/IA might contend that its commitment level warrants four months of continued shared revenue for every twelve months in the alliance. Using the same example as in the solicitor discussion, the CPA/IA continues to receive shared revenue for twenty months after retirement.

Retirement Buyout
Same as a solicitor alliance; there is none because the IA does not own the revenue stream generating his shared fees.

Retirement Example Summary
A CPA firm that has been an IA for five years at 20 percent of fees (average of the 17.5 percent for oversee service and 22.5 percent for advise service), or $30,000 annually ($150,000 times 20 percent), receives twenty months (at four months for every twelve months in the alliance) of continued shared revenue after entering the retirement phase. The sum after twenty months equals $50,000.

Regulatory/Licensing Requirements
The CPA must complete NASD Central Repository Directory (CRD) registration documentation (Form U-4). Upon completion, the CPA is assigned a unique CRD number. The CPA then fulfills state licensing requirements and is placed in the RIA's ADV Part II as an IA. States have different testing requirements, but most want an IA to at least pass the NASD Series 65 test.

Method of Compensation
Sharing the fees generated from managing the assets of those clients the CPA refers to the RIA.

Potential Compensation Amount
Moderately high.

Compliance

The IA must abide by the letter of the RIA's ADV Part II, and all parts of the 1940 Act and its subsequently adopted rules and regulations.

Office Logistics

This is a joint business decision between the CPA and the RIA. There are advantages and disadvantages from both perspectives of the CPA maintaining an office within the RIA's confines. From the CPA's positive view, it might increase CPA business if the members of the RIA firm are affected by his constant presence and refer their clients to him. From the negative side, the CPA's existing client base might find it uncomfortable to visit their CPA inside a setting that is predominately investment-oriented. The RIA certainly would enjoy the revenue from renting an idle office or two. But this could easily develop into a negative: if the RIA signs a lease with a CPA/IA for its final two offices and then a potent, distinguished colleague announces she wants to become a partner with the RIA, there's no office space available.

Client Profile

Same as solicitor alliance; clients with definite investment advice needs; probably not small business owners, unless the RIA pursues the retirement plan market.

Current Entity Size

Sole proprietor.

Current Entity Business Structure

The IA must be a human being. This does not imply that the IA cannot be a member of a business entity—sole proprietor or multi-partnered firm.

Shared-Compensation Flow Inside the CPA Firm

Because the shared revenue of the alliance goes directly to the IA, this does not apply.

Internal Marketing

Because the IA alliance is with a single CPA, this does not apply, unless a multipartnered CPA firm engaged this alliance by licensing one partner. In this case, the routing of the shared revenue after the licensed partner receives it is beyond the scope of the law; she can do anything she wants with it.

Managing Clients' Perceptions

Being part of the RIA's ADV Part II involves the CPA more thoroughly than any previously examined alliance. All alliance clients receive the ADV Part II. The CPA/IA has wide latitude in how he informs clients of the alliance. This is not to imply that the CPA can falsely depict his IA role in the alliance.

The CPA is under no obligation to verbally enlighten the client that the CPA has a presence in the ADV. The client holds the responsibility to read the document. This leaves the CPA with the choice of discussing his role in the alliance upon delivering the ADV or waiting for the client to inquire after reading the ADV. Aside from education, employment, and time committed to being an IA, there is no other information provided about the CPA/IA, including the IA's compensation amount and method. The CPA is under no obligation to reveal information that falls outside these realms. The choice to do so is the CPA's. Possessing this authority means the CPA can manage his clients' perception of the alliance on an individual basis. How to frame the CPA's role in the alliance to the client depends on how it is marketed to the client.

Marketing to Clients

There are three general service styles the sole proprietor CPA might employ as an IA on behalf of his clients: oversee, assist, or advise. With the oversee style, the CPA firm scrutinizes the RIA's investment advice on behalf of the CPA's client and agrees when appropriate or disagrees when necessary. These are actions the CPA can lawfully perform. (Again, if a CPA were not licensed, as in the solicitor alliance, agreement or disagreement with the RIA cannot be expressed in any way to the client. Doing so is tantamount to giving advice, which is reserved for licensed individuals.) With an assist operating style, the CPA participates with the RIA in writing and monitoring the CPA client's investment policy statement, including providing direct input into specific investment decisions. With the advise mode, the CPA becomes the principal adviser for the CPA client, maintaining sole control and responsibility (in consultation with the client) for the client's investment policy statement and coordinating operational requirements with the RIA.

The great advantage of having these three options is the flexibility of matching style to client. Each—oversee, assist, advise—requires a different marketing message to the client, framed with the qualities of each as the CPA sees fit.

Marketing efforts should be significant given the exhaustive registration and licensing process the CPA went through to enter the alliance. The most thorough efforts involve notifying each client by way of "official" announcement that the CPA firm and the RIA have engaged in a strategic alliance that will deliver specific benefits (service styles) to the CPA clients.

CPAs as "Client Advocate"

An IA alliance alters, or adds to, the CPA's role as a financial adviser to the client. Licensing to be an IA in effect, and by law, makes the CPA the client's advocate—but only as an investment adviser. From the CPA position, each service style carries its own degree of client advocacy and most likely its own compensation payout level. The oversee style holds the highest dose of advocacy (and the least compensation) because the CPA is in a monitoring position. The advise style the least advocacy (the highest compensation) because the CPA is the investment adviser. The assist style (and its compensation) falls somewhere between oversee and advise.

Evolutionary Prognosis

This IA alliance is far stronger than that of the solicitor alliance and its longevity more probable. The depth of commitment to the alliance from both sides at the outset goes a great distance in assuring success. The CPA must register with the NASD through the CRD system and become state licensed, all of which represents time and money. The RIA must sponsor and coordinate this entire process. These coordinated activities are a more binding adhesive than a solicitor's agreement that either party can void with a thirty-day notice. The sole proprietor CPA who engages in this alliance has essentially brought his practice to the very brink of merging it with the RIA without actually doing so.

> **INVESTMENT ADVISER'S COMMENT**
> *As a CPA, this is actually a very nice stepping stone to an Active ownership position and potentially merging your practice. It provides you with a ground-level marketing and operational perspective of the RIA business. If you like what you see and it fits with your business model, then pursue an active ownership position.*

If Needed, an Honorable Dissolution

Same as the solicitor alliance, except the IA termination has regulatory elements couched in SEC procedure. The CPA must inform the NASD that it is vacating its CPA/IA registration with the RIA by filing exit documentation called Form U-5. Recall that Form U-4 registers a person with an RIA. Form U-5 officially removes that person from the RIA. After U-5ing out of the RIA, the IA remains part of the CRD system but is unaffiliated with an active body registered with the SEC. Essentially, the CPA/IA is "homeless" until he re-affiliates with another RIA by completing another Form U-4 for that RIA.

Passive (Noncontrolling) Ownership in an RIA

Recall that noncontrolling ownership is an SEC term meaning that an entity holding this position has no decision-making power in any facet of the RIA. This entity can be a CPA sole proprietor or a multipartner firm. If it is a multipartner firm, the individual owners of the CPA firm must be reported in the RIA's ADV Part I as indirect, noncontrolling owners. In addition, the passive owner does not share in the ongoing profits of an RIA, unlike an active owner. However passive owners do reap financial reward when and if the RIA is sold.

Ownership and Structure

Ownership of Revenue Stream

Yes. The passive owner CPA firm claims ownership of the revenue stream generated by the clients it referred to the RIA. It is important to note that this claim on ownership does not originate from the SEC but from the operating agreement of the RIA. Owning the stream of revenue of the CPA referrals can be of great value. The method for determining the value of the revenue stream is discussed in "Shares Owned."

Capital Contribution

Yes. The RIA will probably request that the CPA firm contribute a single specific amount of money to the RIA's balance sheet. Without a capital contribution, the CPA firm, with regards to commitment, becomes nothing more than a solicitor. The purpose of the capital contribution is to move the dedication level well beyond that of the solicitor alliance and even that of the IA alliance. In establishing an alliance, the solicitor spends very little time, the IA spends significant time and effort, and the passive owner spends a lump sum.

The contribution amount depends on two factors (the RIA firm can certainly inject more into the mix): the present value of the amounts previously contributed by the active owners and the SEC's percentage ownership parameters for active owners.

Active ownership, the final choice tackled in the next section, is the pinnacle of strategic alliances and requires substantially greater monetary commitment than all other versions. So it is impractical to expect the passive owner's capital contribution amount to be equal to or in excess of the active owner's amount, adjusted for time and inflation. As well, the RIA, in calculating the passive owner amount, must remember the SEC's definition of an active (controlling) owner—25 percent or more of the RIA itself, irrelevant of voting power.

The combination of the amount of revenue stream owned and the value of the capital contribution, relative to the RIA's totals in each of these categories, is the passive owner's net percentage ownership position in the RIA. This sum cannot be equal to or greater than 25 percent or the passive (noncontrolling) owner becomes, in the eyes of the SEC, an active (controlling) owner.

Shares Owned

A CPA firm assuming a passive ownership position will want documented representation of its claim to ownership of the revenue stream produced by the clients it has referred to the alliance and of its capital contribution. The RIA satisfies this with the issuance of two share classes: Class B (revenue stream) and Class A (capital contribution). The value of one share of each class is equal to one dollar; this never changes. Active and passive owners can hold varying amounts of both classes of shares.

The most fundamental method of determining the number of Class B shares (revenue stream) a passive owner can claim is this: it is equal to the revenue stream generated by those clients referred by the passive owner to the RIA relative to the total revenue stream of the RIA itself. This is a mathematical simplification of what could become a complex calculation depending upon the unique financial propensities of the alliance members.

Here is a revenue stream summary:

Revenue stream from passive owner referrals:	$500,000
Divided by	
The total RIA revenue stream:	$5,000,000
Equals percentage CPA (passive) ownership	10%

Here is a Class B share ownership summary:

The number of Class B shares owned:	500,000
Divided by	
The total RIA outstanding Class B shares	5,000,000
Equals percentage CPA (passive) ownership	10%

This method of ownership valuation is both simple and precise and will serve all owners well when and if the RIA firm is sold.

The combination of Class B share relative value and Class A share absolute value determines the net percentage ownership of the RIA, of both active and passive owners.

Class B share breakdown and percentage of total:

Revenue of clients of active owners	$4,500,000 – 90%
Revenue of clients of CPA (passive owner)	$ 500,000 – 10%
Total Class B shares outstanding	$5,000,000 – 100%

Class A share breakdown and percentage of total:

Capital contribution by active owners	$100,000 – 95.24%
Capital contribution by CPA (passive owner)	5,000 – 4.76%
Total Class A shares outstanding	$105,000 –100.00%

Combined valuation and percentage of total:

Active owners	$4,600,000 – 90.11%
CPA (passive owner)	$ 505,000 – 9.89%
Total combined valuation	$5,105,000 –100.00%

There are two ways to approach the valuation of the RIA if it were sold: Class A share buyback or combined valuation. In the Class A share buyback, the Class A shares are purchased from each owner at the dollar per share value and then individual ownership valuations are calculated using only Class B shares. With the combined valuation method the combined percentage ownership is used to determine individual values.

Let's say the RIA firm above is sold for three times annual revenue, or $15 million. Using the Class A buyback method, the CPA firm would receive $5,000 for the Class A shares (a return of capital contribution) and $1.5 million (10 percent of $15 million) for the Class B shares, totaling $1,505,000. Using the combined method, the CPA firm would receive 9.89 percent of $15 million, or $1,483,500, a difference of $21,500.

Revenue-Sharing Rate

A CPA firm as a passive owner might assume that if the CPA in an IA alliance could negotiate up to a 22.5 percent revenue-sharing rate (advise service level) then it should be able to attain at least that rate. This assumption, as the RIA will probably state, is not correct. The CPA/IA consumed time and money to become licensed, permitting the CPA/IA to dispense investment advice, which carries a degree of liability. Moreover, there is some likelihood that the CPA/IA has located his CPA practice within the offices of the RIA, creating rental income for the RIA.

The CPA firm as a passive owner does not become licensed, cannot provide investment advice, does not shoulder liability, and probably has office space independent of the RIA. And finally, as we see in the "Retirement Example Summary" section, the ownership of the asset management fees that generate the shared revenues ultimately puts the passive owner in a more lucrative position than that of the CPA/IA. With this rationale, the RIA will contend that a base 15 percent payout to the CPA passive owner is reasonable.

RIA Financial Disclosure

The CPA firm is asked to place a lump sum capital contribution onto the balance sheet of the RIA. This gives the CPA firm the right to inspect that balance sheet. As well, in order to assess the future protection of that capital infusion, the CPA firm has the right to review the RIA's profit and loss statement.

Noncompete Agreement

Same as the solicitor alliance. The CPA firm could dissolve the existing alliance and resurface in an alliance with another RIA and begin siphoning the clients it referred to the original RIA. Because of a stake in the ownership of the asset management fee base that generates the shared revenue, an arbitrary departure of a CPA passive owner is unlikely. Nonetheless, personality conflicts can prompt strange and poor decisions, and the RIA must protect itself from such instances.

RIA Employee
The passive owner is not an employee but an investor in the RIA.

Voting Rights
None.

Legalities
Passive Owner agreement, which includes a noncompete clause.

Tax Reporting
Partnership K-1 tax form.

RIA Approval
Majority vote is required from active partners.

Retirement Trigger
Buyout can occur upon request of the CPA passive owner. The RIA might consider attaching stipulations regarding a minimum number of referrals in a given period, much as the solicitor alliance and the IA alliance do, that would automatically flip the buyout trigger. On the other hand, the CPA firm might contend that because it owns the fee stream of those referred clients, a fee stream that will grow with the market, it cannot be forced to sell it. Time to negotiate.

Retirement Payout Period
Negotiated, based on the total amount paid out. Both members of the alliance must evaluate cash flow needs and arrive at a suitable period for the buyout of the managed asset base delivered by the CPA during the life of the alliance.

Retirement Buyout
The next section shows that a CPA firm, as an active owner, will claim 75 percent ownership of the asset stream of the clients it referred to the alliance. The passive owner, maintaining a less significant role in the daily business activities of the RIA, has an equally less significant ownership stake. This smaller percentage is a number the RIA must

arrive at internally, but should allow for some negotiating wiggle room. For the purposes of the "Retirement Example Summary," 50 percent is used.

Retirement Example Summary

A CPA firm that has been a passive owner for five years at 15 percent of fees, or $22,500 ($150,000 times 15 percent) annually, receives 50 percent of the value of the revenue base of $150,000, or $75,000, paid out over three years at $25,000 per year.

Regulatory/Licensing Requirements

The CPA must be listed as a noncontrolling owner in the RIA's ADV Part I, which is not provided to clients. If the CPA is a firm, or creates a new entity to accommodate the alliance, and that firm is the noncontrolling owner, then each member of the firm must be listed in the ADV Part I as indirect noncontrolling owners. The CPA firm members are not licensed and cannot provide investment advice to clients.

Method of Compensation

Sharing the fees generated from managing the assets of those clients the CPA refers to the RIA.

Potential Compensation Amount

High.

Compliance

Because the CPA passive owner is listed as a noncontrolling owner in the ADV Part I, and is merely a conduit for referrals, there are no compliance issues, other than the fact the CPA passive owner cannot give investment advice.

> INVESTMENT ADVISER'S COMMENT
> *Informing the client or potential client of the CPA's passive ownership position is entirely up to the CPA.*

Office Logistics

Unless either member of the alliance is a sole proprietor, it is unlikely that either one would maintain an office within the confines of the other member's offices. The main purpose for sharing office space, or at least maintaining an office presence within the other member's offices, is to eliminate the out-of-sight, out-of-mind syndrome. In an ownership alliance where the CPA firm provides a capital contribution, this syndrome is unlikely to arise.

Client Profile

Same as the solicitor alliance and the IA alliance.

Current Entity Size

The size of the CPA firm is important only in the potential size of the referral stream: the larger the firm, the larger the stream.

Current Entity Business Structure

This is relevant only if, as mentioned above, the CPA firm itself becomes the passive owner in the alliance. This would require that each owner of the CPA firm be listed as indirect, noncontrolling owners on the RIA's ADV Part I.

Shared-Compensation Flow Inside the CPA Firm

The flow of compensation after the CPA firm receives it from the RIA is at the firm's discretion and has no regulatory restrictions.

Internal Marketing

This should be an unnecessary exercise. Internal marketing is rendered moot by the decision itself to engage in a passive ownership alliance with an RIA. There should be no need to persuade the CPA firm partners to participate by referring clients to the RIA. If the alliance entity is the CPA firm itself or a created entity, all members will participate.

Example: If a CPA firm has seven partners and only five believe a passive owner alliance with the RIA is favorable, the five CPAs cannot use the CPA firm as a receptacle for the shared revenue because the two dissenting partners would benefit. A separate business entity should be created, owned by the five willing partners. In effect, all members of the CPA entity in the alliance will refer clients, whether it's 100 percent of the partners of the CPA firm itself or 100 percent of the partners of a specially created entity. Therefore, no internal marketing is necessary.

Managing Clients' Perceptions

The attributes of this task are very similar to those of the CPA/IA alliance just discussed. As a passive owner, the CPA firm is listed in the RIA's ADV Part I. Thus, the alliance itself and all its surrounding details can remain private. The CPA firm has complete discretion as to what facts, if any, it wants to divulge to its clients about the alliance. As with the CPA/IA alliance, controlling this information allows the CPA firm to tailor each client's individual perception of the alliance.

Marketing to Clients

If the CPA firm takes the position that the alliance should remain private, then the concerted marketing of the alliance will not occur. The CPA firm will merely urge clients to consult with the RIA. Because there is monetary commitment to the alliance by the CPA firm, the vigor and frequency of these recommendations should be robust.

CPAs as "Client Advocate"

As with the solicitor alliance, the CPA passive owner cannot act as advocate by giving its opinion on investment advice provided by the RIA. This is tantamount to giving advice, behavior for which the CPA passive owner is not licensed. Advocacy can be maintained on ancillary, noninvestment factors of the RIA.

In the discussion of the CPA firm in a solicitor alliance, the position taken is that nonownership is the more appropriate structure to maintain objectivity because the CPA firm has no claim on the revenue stream of the RIA. However, an opposing view might be that just such a claim to ownership enhances client advocacy. Holding ownership of a portion of the RIA's revenue stream, the CPA passive owner will want to ensure the clients remain happy and the RIA remains viable.

Evolutionary Prognosis

The saying "time is money" equates the two. But "money is money" leaves no doubt. A passive owner CPA must place a capital contribution (money is money) on the table to engage the RIA in an alliance. This makes the passive ownership alliance more durable than the CPA/IA alliance or any alliance discussed thus far. As seen in previous "Evolutionary Prognosis" discussions, the more deeply dedicated the CPA is to the alliance, either with time or money, the longer its life and the more potent its profit. The passive ownership position is the most sturdy of all alliance choices without becoming an active, controlling owner of the RIA itself, which is reviewed in a moment.

If the CPA passive owner is a multipartner firm, the alliance longevity is related to the long-term business continuity of the firm itself. As long as both the RIA and the CPA firm remain solvent and add new partners or replace retired ones, the alliance should remain strong and profitable.

If the passive owner CPA is a sole proprietor who retires from professional accounting practice while still a passive owner, the alliance continuity does not have to suffer or end. In fact, it might become more powerful. The retiring CPA might encounter more potential referrals during retirement activities (golf, trips, etc.) than during the days of his practice. A prerequisite of being a passive owner, CPA or otherwise, should not be that the individual is actively employed.

If Needed, an Honorable Dissolution

The passive ownership alliance can disintegrate for similar reasons reviewed in other alliance discussions: the passive owner or member of the passive owner gives investment advice, for which she is not licensed; poor business practices of the RIA; the CPA firm lacks serious commitment; there is a personality conflict.

In the solicitor and IA alliance dissolutions, the CPA firm moved into the retirement phase upon dissolution. In the passive owner-ship alliance, the RIA buys from the CPA firm the revenue stream that generates the shared revenue according to the provisions in the buyout agreement. However, unlike the (unlicensed) solicitor, who would not enter the retirement phase and continue receiving shared revenue if it violated the 1940 Act by giving investment advice, the passive owner who violated the Act would still be entitled to the pro-visions of the buyout agreement. The passive owner CPA owns the revenue stream; the solicitor does not.

Active (Controlling) Ownership in an RIA

According to the SEC, a controlling owner of an RIA either has vot-ing rights on any issue regarding the operation of the RIA or owns more than 25 percent of the RIA. The owner can be a CPA sole proprietor or a multipartner firm. If the owner is a multipartner firm, the individual owners of the CPA firm must be reported in the RIA's ADV Part I as indirect, controlling owners.

Ownership and Structure

Ownership of Revenue Stream

Yes. In the passive ownership alliance, the CPA firm owns only the revenue stream of clients it referred to the alliance. The active owner has an alternative, depending upon the general objective and the structure of the alliance. There are two means of structuring the alli-ance: integration and newborn.

With integration, the CPA firm becomes an active owner of the existing RIA. With the newborn method, the CPA firm and the active owners of the existing RIA form a jointly owned separate RIA that then notifies the SEC it is dissolving the original RIA.

Integrating the CPA firm into the RIA as an active owner is the cleanest and easiest method. Like the previous three RIA alliances, the shared revenue is determined by the revenue generated from the clients referred to the alliance from the day the CPA firm is reported as an active owner on the RIA's ADV Part I. The calculation of own-ership value is very straightforward. As a result of integration, clauses in the RIA's existing operating agreement might become obsolete or irrelevant and require revision through addendums.

A newborn alliance presents an array of revenue ownership possibilities and requires the compilation of an entirely new operation agreement. Many of the factors in this "Ownership and Structure" section are normally addressed to some degree in the operating agreement. For each following factor, when necessary, each structure—integration and newborn—is discussed separately.

Capital Contribution

Yes. If the structure is integration, the capital contribution should be equal to the amount contributed by the original active owners, adjusted for a growth factor, either an opportunity-lost percentage, like the S&P 500 index, or inflation.

If the structure is newborn, the total capital contribution should be equal to working capital needs for the projected number of months the firm will be without asset management fee revenue. These are funds necessary to launch the new alliance and to ensure its first months of operation are on sound financial footing. Each member of the alliance provides the amount of capital based on the agreed-upon percentage share of ownership of the alliance itself.

Shares Owned

Class A Shares

You may remember that capital contributions are represented by Class A shares, at a fixed dollar-per-share. However, they are ultimately insignificant relative to individual active Class B shares, which are based on the asset management revenue stream each owner (passive or active) brings to the RIA alliance. It can be written in the operating agreement that Class A shares can be repurchased by the RIA at some time in the future when sufficient working capital is supplied by the asset management revenue base.

If the RIA is mature and operates comfortably on its fee-based revenue, the capital contribution by a CPA firm active owner becomes more a gesture of commitment than one of needed cash infusion.

Class B Shares

Class B shares represent active ownership, again at one dollar per share. But Class B shares are not fixed in value, as are Class A shares. For every dollar of asset management fee an owner (active or passive) brings to the alliance, it (or he or she) owns one Class B share. Class B shares represent performance-based ownership. The more fee-generating assets an owner adds to the RIA, the more of the RIA that owner claims.

Following is an example of Class A and Class B ownership involving original owners and an alliance with a CPA firm.

Four active owners start an RIA, each contributing $25,000 in capital, giving each 25,000 Class A shares. Six years later, the RIA adds a reputable CPA firm as an active owner. The capital contribution of the CPA firm is $29,851 ($25,000 six years later at 3 percent inflation). The CPA active owner possesses 29,851 Class A shares. Adding these shares to the original active owners' total of 100,000 shares means there are 129,851 of outstanding Class A shares. At one dollar per share, the total amount of value in Class A shares is $129,851.

Here's a summary of Class A share value and the ownership percentages before accepting the CPA firm as an active partner:

Capital contribution by active owner 1	$ 25,000 – 25%
Capital contribution by active owner 2	$ 25,000 – 25%
Capital contribution by active owner 3	$ 25,000 – 25%
Capital contribution by active owner 4	$ 25,000 – 25%
Total Class A shares outstanding	$100,000 – 100%

Now the impact of accepting the CPA firm on Class A share valuation and percentage of ownership:

Capital contribution by active owner 1	$ 25,000 – 19.25%
Capital contribution by active owner 2	$ 25,000 – 19.25%
Capital contribution by active owner 3	$ 25,000 – 19.25%
Capital contribution by active owner 4	$ 25,000 – 19.25%
Capital contribution by CPA active owner	$ 29,851 – 22.99%
Total Class A shares outstanding	$129,851 – 100.00%

Notice the dilution of the original owners' relative total. The value of Class A shares dropped from 25 percent to 19.25 percent. In fact, the CPA firm's percentage ownership is higher than that of the original owners. As we see in a minute, this small disparity becomes microscopic when combined with the valuation of Class B shares.

From the time of the RIA's inception, each of the original owners has added a specific amount of managed assets that generate fee revenue. As with any group of individuals, some are more skilled at relationship development and/or persuasion. The table below demonstrates the fees generated from the clients brought to the RIA by each owner, including the CPA firm.

Class B share breakdown and percentage of total:

Client revenue of active owner 1	$ 750,000 –	15%
Client revenue of active owner 2	$ 1,000,000 –	20%
Client revenue of active owner 3	$ 2,150,000 –	43%
Client revenue of active owner 4	$ 600,000 –	12%
Client revenue of CPA active owner	$ 500,000 –	10%
Total Class B shares outstanding	$5,000,000 –	100%

The CPA firm's $500,000 is not the revenue amount the CPA firm receives. It is the fee basis by which the revenue sharing rate is multiplied. The values of both class shares are simply added together to determine each owner's amount and percentage ownership of the RIA firm. Below is a table that demonstrates these values assuming the CPA firm's capital contribution was calculated as a present value of the $25,000 capital contribution of the original owners, or at $29,851.

Combined valuation and diluted percentage of total:

Active owner 1	$ 775,000 –	15.11%
Active owner 2	$1,025,000 –	19.98%
Active owner 3	$2,175,000 –	42.40%
Active owner 4	$ 625,000 –	12.18%
CPA active owner	$ 529,851 –	10.33%
Total combined valuation	$5,129,851 –	100.00%

However, if the original owners are uncomfortable with this dilution, they can allow the CPA firm to take its ownership position at the same capital contribution as the original owners.

Combined valuation and nondiluted percentage of total:

Active owner 1	$ 775,000 – 15.12%
Active owner 2	$1,025,000 – 20.00%
Active owner 3	$2,175,000 – 42.44%
Active owner 4	$ 625,000 – 12.20%
CPA active owner	$ 525,000 – 10.24%
Total combined valuation	$5,125,000 – 100.00%

Class A share capital contribution amounts have minimal impact on the net amount of ownership in an RIA. Ownership relies heavily on Class B shares, which makes this structure a performance-based valuation model. Owner 3 has added more assets under management, generating more asset management fees, than any of the other owners and therefore owns more than twice as much of the RIA as owner 2.

If these results change ownership positions materially within a calendar year, they must be recorded in the RIA's ADV Part I. It's up to the RIA's chief compliance officer to determine what is "material" and how often the valuations must be calculated. With proper software and tracking, calculating these ownership valuations is not difficult.

Nonperforming owners

A nonperforming owner of an RIA alliance is one whose primary role is not that of establishing and maintaining client relationships, which produces the firm's revenue. The CPA firm probably has no such owners; it's likely that all CPA owners are business developers and therefore revenue generators. But that might not be the case with an RIA. In many instances an RIA will have owners who cannot claim a revenue stream and thus, according to the performance-based model, would own zero percent of the firm and of any unassigned (profit) revenue. These owners might perform functions such as investment director, a person responsible for creating, monitoring, and remodeling client portfolios when necessary, or the firm's business manager.

In these cases, the performance-based ownership model must be adjusted to provide involvement in ownership for nonperforming owners. Although there are numerous ways of accomplishing this, one strategy is examined in particular detail.

One simple method is "volume redistribution" and is based on the amount of time and energy exerted by the nonperforming owner on tending to the fixed tasks created by the volume of revenue generated by the performance-based owners. In other words, Owner 3, because of the volume of operational work required to maintain his $2,150,000 of fee revenue, will have more ownership and unassigned revenue stripped away from his 43 percent Class B share value and redistributed to the nonperforming owners. At 10 percent, the CPA active owner will forfeit the least amount.

First, the operating agreement must establish what percentage of ownership the nonperforming owners will receive. Two methods might be considered: 1) a set amount or 2) an average of the performing owners' percentage positions of Class B shares. Let's take a look at an example of the second method.

To arrive at the average, throw out the highest and lowest Class B ownership percentages: Owner 3 at 43 percent and the CPA active owner at 10 percent. The average of the remaining owners is 15.67 percent (20 percent, 15 percent, 12 percent). Assume the RIA alliance has two nonperforming owners: an investment director and a compliance officer. Each would receive a 15.67 percent ownership stake and the same claim to any unassigned revenue (profits). This means 31.34 percent of all the performing owners' stakes must be redistributed.

Adjustment amount of performing owners:

Active owner 1	15% x 31.34% = 4.70%
Active owner 2	20% x 31.34% = 6.27%
Active owner 3	43% x 31.34% = 13.48%
Active owner 4	12% x 31.34% = 3.76%
CPA active owner	10% x 31.34% = 3.13%
Total	= 31.34%

This 31.34 percent is stripped from the performing owners by

individually adjusted percentages and is distributed to the two non-performing owners, which creates an entirely new Class B share ownership structure.

Redistribution ownership positions:

Active owner 1	15% − 4.70% =	10.30%
Active owner 2	20% − 6.27% =	13.73%
Active owner 3	43% −13.48% =	29.52%
Active owner 4	12% − 3.76% =	8.24%
CPA active owner	10% − 3.13% =	6.87%
Investment director	0% +15.67% =	15.67%
Compliance officer	0% +15.67% =	15.67%
Total		= 100.00%

Notice this redistribution catapults the two nonperforming owners into solid second and third place ownership positions. One must consider, however, that the cash flow compensation of the nonperforming active owners is limited, whereas the performing owners' compensation has unlimited upside. The impact of this is reviewed in the "Revenue-Sharing Rate" section.

There is an age-old debate about whether nonperforming positions are worthy of such ownership strength. To each firm its own.

Fixed ownership

Take care to avoid a fifty-fifty ownership of the alliance, or some other total fixed ownership based on factors other than assets brought into the RIA firm by individual owners. Doing so locks ownership at 100 percent among originating owners and prevents a simple method of adding passive and active owners, both of which can be significant revenue growth engines.

If a fixed ownership is established at the RIA's outset, adding more owners will require a rewrite of the operating agreement, a costly and time-consuming exercise, or the establishment of a separate RIA entity that houses the original RIA plus the new CPA active owner. It is inside this latter entity that relative ownership can be created by using Class A and Class B shares.

Revenue-Sharing Rate

The revenue-sharing rate of a CPA active owner is an entirely different creature than that of the other three alliances. The amount of revenue not consumed by the designated rate falls to the RIA's bottom line as profit, net of expenses. In most cases, each active owner, including the CPA firm, is entitled to a portion of this profit equal to the combined value of both share classes. The smaller the sharing rate, the more each owner shares in the others' revenue base at the RIA's bottom line.

General example:

Active owner revenue sharing rate	= 15%
RIA alliance expense	= 50%
Profit	**= 35%**

If each active owner receives 15 percent of the revenue stream up front, and 50 percent of the stream is consumed by the expense of operations, that leaves 35 percent of gross revenue as profit, to be shared by the active owners based on each of their combined class share percentage ownership. For active owners with less than 15 percent total ownership, this arrangement is mathematically unfavorable—but only on ownership, not on regular compensation. When ownership of unassigned revenue (net profits) is combined with active owners' personal income from the RIA, the total income of the performing owners is higher than that of the nonperforming owners.

Let's continue with the example from the previous section. Recall that Class B shares, dollar per share, represent the amount of revenue for which each active owner of the RIA alliance is responsible. Assume the operating agreement states that each owner receives 15 percent of the revenue stream as personal income.

Personal income based on Class B share ownership:

Client revenue of active owner 1 =	$ 750,000 x 15% = $ 112,500
Client revenue of active owner 2 =	$1,000,000 x 15% = $150,000
Client revenue of active owner 3 =	$ 2,150,000 x 15% = $322,500
Client revenue of active owner 4 =	$ 600,000 x 15% = $ 90,000
Client revenue of CPA active owner =	$ 500,000 x 15% = $ 75,000
Total revenue and owner income =	**$5,000,000 x 15% = $750,000**

According to the basic calculation above, this deposits $1,750,000 to the RIA's bottom line as net profit:

$2,500,000 (operating expenses)
$ 750,000 (15% revenue-sharing rate paid as personal income)
_____

$1,750,000 (net profit)

Each active owner claims a portion of this net profit based on the redistributed percentage ownership rate. Again, from the example above:

Net profit ownership based on redistribution positions:

Active owner 1	10.30% x $1,750,000 = $ 180,250
Active owner 2	13.73% x $1,750,000 = $ 240,275
Active owner 3	29.52% x $1,750,000 = $ 516,600
Active owner 4	8.24% x $1,750,000 = $ 144,200
CPA active owner	6.87% x $1,750,000 = $ 120,225
Investment director	15.67% x $1,750,000 = $ 274,225
Compliance officer	15.67% x $1,750,000 = $ 274,225
Total	100.00% = $1,750,000

Combine ownership of net profit with that of each active owner's personal income from the RIA:

Total personal income from the RIA alliance:

Active owner 1	$112,500 + $ 180,250 = $ 292,750
Active owner 2	$150,000 + $ 240,275 = $ 390,275
Active owner 3	$322,500 + $ 516,600 = $ 839,100
Active owner 4	$ 90,000 + $ 144,200 = $ 234,200
CPA active owner	$ 75,000 + $ 120,225 = $ 195,225
Investment director	$ 75,000* + $ 274,225 = $ 349,225
Compliance officer	$ 75,000* + $ 274,225 = $ 349,225
Total	$900,000* + $1,750,000 = $2,650,000

*Salary, included in totals.

Notice that the nonperforming owners' total compensation is similar to the other active partners, with the exception of the low-performing owner 4 and the CPA owner. The revenue-sharing rate can be used to bring these compensations somewhat parallel. If the rate is increased the nonperforming owners receive less compensation because there is less that sinks to the bottom line.

RIA Financial Disclosure
Same as the passive owner, except the CPA firm as an active voting owner has a much stronger justification to view the RIA's financials before agreeing to engage in such an intimate alliance.

Noncompete Agreement
Same as the passive owner alliance, except both the RIA and the CPA firm should sign noncompete agreements. Either entity could end the alliance and begin siphoning the clients it referred to the original RIA into a new entity or alliance. The chances of personality conflicts are higher in an active ownership alliance because the CPA firm, and its partners, share decision making with the owners of RIA. Such close quarters can spark friction and potential separation. Both parties need the protection of a noncompete agreement.

RIA Employee
This depends on the type of new business entity chosen or the existing business entity of the RIA, if the CPA firm joins it as an owner.

Voting Rights
Yes, but in what capacity? In the "Shares Owned" section above, active owner 3 owns more than four times (42.44 percent) the RIA than the active CPA owner (10.24 percent). Does active owner 3 have four times the voting power of the CPA owner? Yes and no.

A poor decision can threaten the RIA's quality of service and thus client revenue stream, so owner 3 stands to lose the most from a momentous blunder. Furthermore, as with the sharing of unassigned revenue (profits), the cost of operating the RIA is allocated according to ownership percentage. Owner 3 bears the highest burden of decisions that might increase the firm's expenses.

To alleviate this discrepancy, the operating agreement should define two types of votes: weighted and singular. Weighted votes are exercised on financial decisions with a specific spending ceiling and are based on ownership percentages. A singular vote is on nonfinancial matters and each owner possesses one vote. An RIA's operating agreement might state that any decision to spend over $15,000 is determined by a weighted vote; all other decisions are by singular vote. For example: an RIA must make two decisions: 1) to purchase a new computer server and update all software at a cost of $22,000 and 2) to change health insurance providers that will not change premium costs. Decision 1 is a weighted vote, and owner 3, in conjunction with any other single owner, will make the decision. Decision 2 is singular and all owners cast equal votes.

Legalities

Operating agreement. There is either an existing operating agreement or a need to create one. If an RIA's operating agreement was compiled for growth through alliances, a CPA firm (or any similar financial entity) will be able to slide seamlessly into an active ownership position within the RIA. The primary ingredient of an operating agreement written for growth is performance-based ownership as opposed to fixed ownership (fifty-fifty, seventy-thirty, eighty-twenty, etc.), which severely restricts growth. Percentage of ownership is usually set at the beginning of a fixed ownership RIA and is commonly determined in two ways: arbitrary (usually resulting in fifty-fifty) or Class A shares only (the amount of capital contribution). Certainly, the operating agreement clauses that stipulate fixed ownership can be altered, by dilution, to allow for the insertion of the CPA firm as a new owner. But the CPA firm, as with the existing owners, becomes a fixed owner itself. The basic problem remains: the valuation of ownership is not determined by performance.

One critical factor could devastate a CPA firm alliance unless it is thoroughly addressed in the operating agreement: the treatment of revenue (current and future) from the RIA's existing clients. Ownership percentages should not apply to this revenue stream as the CPA firm had no part in bringing the clients to the previous RIA.

If an RIA entity is created to house the new alliance, the previous RIA client revenue (current and future) should be excluded from ownership valuations, whether fixed or performance-based.

Tax Reporting
Depends on employee status. An IRS Form 1099 will be issued to partners, W-4 to employees.

RIA Approval
A majority vote of the current active partners.

Buyout Trigger
At the request of any active owner.

Buyout Period
Same as the passive owner, except the period should be stipulated in the operating agreement.

Buyout Provisions
Same as the passive owner, except instead of payout based on 50 percent ownership of the revenue stream, the active owner might receive 75 percent. Whatever percentage is employed, it should be stipulated in the operating agreement.

Buyout Example
A CPA firm that has been an active owner for five years at 15 percent of fees, or $22,500 ($150,000 times 15 percent) annually, receives 75 percent of the value of the revenue base of $150,000, or $112,500, paid out over four years at $28,125 per year.

Regulatory/Licensing Requirements
Same as the passive owner, except instead of being listed as a noncontrolling owner, the CPA firm must be listed as a controlling owner in the RIA's ADV Part I, which is not distributed to clients.

Method of Compensation

Sharing fees generated by the clients the CPA firm brings to the alliance.

Potential Compensation Amount

Very high.

Compliance

As a controlling owner of an RIA, the CPA firm (or the entity it creates for the alliance) must abide by all information in the ADV Part II and by all parts of the 1940 Act. In addition, no member of the CPA firm can give investment advice without first passing required tests.

Office Logistics

The new alliance owners should share office space. The out-of-sight, out-of-mind syndrome can easily hinder the growth of the alliance, and perhaps eventually destroy it.

Client Profile

Same as the solicitor, IA, and passive owner alliances.

Current Entity Size

Same as the passive owner.

Current Entity Business Structure

The most desirable structure is the creation by the CPA firm of a new and separate entity that would enter the RIA alliance. If the CPA firm is multipartnered and one partner votes against the alliance, a new and separate entity must be created if the remaining partners want to pursue the alliance; those partners would become the owners (or partners) of the new entity, carving out the lone dissenter.

If the existing RIA has a fixed ownership structure, the CPA firm might strongly suggest that a second RIA be created where ownership is performance-based, with the initial RIA and the newly created CPA entity as the only two owners. Doing this also allows the operating agreement of the new RIA to be freshly compiled, thereby accommodating future alliances with other professional entities.

Shared-Compensation Flow Inside the CPA Firm

The compensation flow would be the same as with the passive owner structure. In addition, realizing unassigned revenues (profits) is a business function unaffected by regulatory issues.

Internal Marketing

As is the case with the passive owner structure, this function is successfully accomplished during the CPA firm's due diligence and subsequent debate on the prospects of entering the alliance. If the vote is yes, unanimous or otherwise, internal marketing is completed.

Managing Clients' Perceptions

Although the alliance is described in the RIA's ADV Part I, which clients don't see, the CPA firm has made a major decision to legally join forces with an RIA and probably ought to disclose the general outlines of the alliance to its clients. If the CPA firm desired privacy, it would have been better served in a passive alliance.

The relationship between the activities of a CPA and an RIA are symbiotic and it's easy to make the case that an alliance which provides additional and higher quality service to the CPA firm's clients is not challenging. The relationship will be even stronger if the alliance members share office space. From the client's perspective, proximity begets convenience and efficiency.

Marketing to Clients

This is where the alliance should spend a large part of those capital contributions. Marketing the new alliance to the CPA firm's current clients should be a pervasive and persistent effort involving personal meetings, letters of introduction, in-house seminars, dinners for A-level clients, and media attention.

Marketing to future clients involves simply extolling the benefits of the alliance while walking the prospect down the hall for an introduction to the members of the RIA.

CPAs as "Client Advocate"

This issue is the same as that of internal marketing to the CPA firm's partners. As an active (controlling) owner of an RIA alliance, the issue of the CPA firm as client advocate is settled when the CPA firm debates whether to even engage in the alliance and during the due diligence process. If the CPA partners believe client advocacy will be violated if they enter the alliance, they should not do so.

Evolutionary Prognosis

This is thorny. On the one hand the alliance parties are business partners, which weaves them together tightly and legally. On the other hand, this very intimate daily interaction will eventually expose raw philosophical and personality conflicts, which can weaken and perhaps eventually destroy the alliance.

To avoid or at least mitigate the latter, the alliance members should engage each other and attempt to unearth and discuss these possible tensions early in the relationship. The alliance might also consider including in the operating agreement an arbitration clause, where any entity-threatening disputes are resolved by an arbitrator, perhaps a mutually respected attorney.

If these menacing conditions are recognized and dealt with as early as possible, their destructive power is diminished and there is a very good chance the active ownership alliance will be enduring.

If Needed, an Honorable Dissolution

If the parties agree to separate, there are various steps that must be taken, depending on how the alliance was originally structured—either as a new RIA entity or as the CPA firm becoming an active owner of the existing RIA.

New RIA Entity

There are three fundamental steps that occur if the alliance was begun as a new RIA entity, owned by the CPA and the existing RIA, and is discontinued. First is the suspension of the business entity. The second is to dissolve the RIA, a definitive SEC process, unless either party negotiates with the other to keep it intact. The third is finding an investment home for the alliance clients. The first two steps are procedural and clear. The third step is not, and because it involves money, it can get ugly. Remember, if the entity dies, so does the operating agreement and with it, the noncompete stipulation. Clients and their assets are now fair game for either member of the dying entity.

Recall that one of the owners of the dissolving alliance is an RIA itself, the original one. The act of moving the clients of the dying RIA to the original RIA is a simple task, especially if both RIAs used the same custodian and/or institutional brokerage firm, a likely scenario. In such a case, the original RIA must merely provide the client with its ADV Part II, also probably not much different from the one used by the dissolving RIA, and have new investment policy contracts signed by the exiting clients. (The institutional brokerage firm might require new applications signed as well.) Also, the core business of the RIA is to dispense investment advice and subsequently manage assets. The clients are very likely to view this as a seamless and logical transition.

These conditions put the CPA firm at a disadvantage, especially if none of the members of the CPA firm are licensed with their domiciled state to give investment advice. There are two alternatives: 1) become an RIA or 2) align with another RIA. Both these choices promise greater disadvantages than advantages.

In the first instance, at least one CPA member must scramble to become licensed by studying for and passing at least one test, perhaps two, a process that could take a few months. In the meantime the alliance structurally and legally is being dismantled; it's not likely that the exiting RIA is going to loiter while the CPA firm becomes legitimate. Clients of the dying alliance will question the expertise of the freshly licensed CPA members.

In the second instance, the CPA firm must execute due diligence on the RIA it is reviewing, a time-consuming process. Furthermore, the transition from one RIA to another requires the completion of extensive documentation by the RIA and the client.

The CPA Firm as an Owner in the Existing RIA

If the alliance was formed when the CPA firm became an active owner of the original RIA, there are two steps to dissolution. The first is to remove the CPA firm as an owner from the RIA's ADV Part I and re-file with the SEC. The second step is similar to the third step above: what to do with the alliance clients. The CPA firm is at a greater disadvantage with this alliance structure. The alliance clients are already clients of the original RIA. The CPA firm still has the same two options it had under the new entity structure. But persuading clients to wade through all the new documentation to change to an unknown, when the alternative is to do nothing and continue receiving the same investment advice, would be a very daunting task.

In Summary

A CPA firm considering an alliance with an RIA has four options of how that alliance will be structured: solicitor, investment adviser (IA), passive owner, and active owner. The CPA firm might not have all four of these options offered to it by the RIA. For internal reasons, the RIA might offer only one or two options, most likely the solicitor or the IA options (if the CPA is a sole proprietor).

The RIA will have specific criteria that it applies to a CPA firm before offering it either the passive or active ownership status. Meeting the conditions of passive ownership will likely be less demanding than meeting those of active ownership, which requires thorough business integration of the RIA and the CPA firm.

Retirement/Buyout Example Summary

Below is a comparison of how a retirement or buyout might be handled in the different strategic alliance structures. In our example, the CPA has referred clients with assets of $15 million to the RIA. At a 1 percent annual management fee, these assets are producing $150,000 of fees.

A CPA firm that has been a solicitor for five years at 15 percent of fees, or $22,500 annually ($150,000 times 15 percent), receives ten months (at two months for every twelve months in the alliance) of continued shared revenue after entering the retirement phase. The sum after ten months equals $18,750.

A CPA firm that has been an IA for five years at 20 percent of fees (average of the 17.5 percent for oversee service and 22.5 percent for advise service), or $30,000 annually ($150,000 times 20 percent), receives twenty months (at four months for every twelve months in the alliance) of continued shared revenue after entering the retirement phase. The sum after twenty months equals $50,000.

A CPA firm that has been a passive owner for five years at 15 percent of fees, or $22,500 ($150,000 times 15 percent) annually, receives 50 percent of the value of the revenue base of $150,000, or $75,000, paid out over three years at $25,000 per year.

A CPA firm that has been an active owner for five years at 15 percent of fees, or $22,500 ($150,000 times 15 percent) annually, receives 75 percent of the value of the revenue base of $150,000, or $112,500, paid out over four years at $28,125 per year.

In all of these retirement phase/buyout structures the RIA is paying out a rough average of $26,000 per year while collecting $150,000 per year from the CPA's referred clients, not including growth of the asset base. As well, from the CPA's perspective, moving from the choice of minimal commitment (solicitor) to the choice of maximum commitment (active owner), the total payout to the CPA also moves from the least ($18,750) to the most ($112,500).

A Multiowner Alliance RIA: Quantitative Analysis

Following is an expanded illustration of the alliance ownership positions discussed above. The facts of the ownership structure:

◆ Four individuals start the RIA with capital contributions of $25,000 each
◆ Passive owner capital contribution is fixed at $10,000
◆ Three years later an alliance is established with passive owner 1
◆ Three years after that a CPA firm is added as an active owner
◆ Two years later a second passive owner alliance is established
◆ The following year a business benefits group is added as an active owner

♦ The diluted method of valuing Class A shares is employed, using 3 percent inflation

Over the course of this time, three solicitor alliances are formed and four investment advisers are hired.

Capital contributions (Class A share value and percentage of ownership):

Original active owner 1	$ 25,000 – 13.70%
Original active owner 2	$ 25,000 – 13.70%
Original active owner 3	$ 25,000 – 13.70%
Original active owner 4	$ 25,000 – 13.70%
Passive owner alliance 1	$ 10,000 – 5.48%
CPA firm active owner alliance	$ 29,851 – 16.36%
Passive owner alliance 2	$ 10,000 – 5.48%
Benefits group active owner alliance	$ 32,619 – 17.88%
Three solicitors	$ 0 – 0%
Four IAs	$ 0 – 0%
Total Class A shares outstanding	**$182,470 – 100.00%**

Client fees generated (Class B share value and percentage of ownership):

Client revenue of active owner 1	$ 750,000 – 11.86%
Client revenue of active owner 2	$1,000,000 – 15.81%
Client revenue of active owner 3	$2,150,000 – 33.99%
Client revenue of active owner 4	$ 600,000 – 9.49%
Passive owner alliance 1	$ 800,000 – 12.65%
CPA firm active owner alliance	$ 500,000 – 7.91%
Passive owner alliance 2	$ 350,000 – 5.53%
Benefits group active owner alliance	$ 175,000 – 2.77%
Three solicitors	$ 0 – 0%
Four IAs	$ 0 – 0%
Total Class B shares	**$6,325,000 – 100.0%**

Combined valuation of Class A and Class B shares and percentage total:

Client revenue of active owner 1	$ 775,000 –	11.91%
Client revenue of active owner 2	$1,025,000 –	15.75%
Client revenue of active owner 3	$2,175,000 –	33.42%
Client revenue of active owner 4	$ 625,000 –	9.60%
Passive owner alliance 1	$ 810,000 –	12.45%
CPA firm active owner alliance	$ 529,851 –	8.14%
Passive owner alliance 2	$ 360,000 –	5.53%
Benefits group active owner alliance	$ 207,619 –	3.19%
Three solicitors	$ 0 –	0%
Four IAs	$ 0 –	0%
Total combined valuation	**$6,507,470 –**	**100.00%**

Combining the revenue of all owners with that of the solicitors and the IAs gives the RIA's total annual revenue.

Total RIA fee revenue and percentage ownership:

Active owner 1	$ 750,000 –	11.86%
Active owner 2	$1,000,000 –	15.81%
Active owner 3	$2,150,000 –	33.99%
Active owner 4	$ 600,000 –	9.49%
Passive owner alliance 1	$ 800,000 –	12.65%
CPA firm active owner alliance	$ 500,000 –	7.91%
Passive owner alliance 2	$ 350,000 –	5.53%
Benefits group active owner alliance	$ 175,000 –	2.77%
Three solicitors	$ 600,000 –	0%
Four IAs	$3,000,000 –	0%
Total fee revenue & percentage ownership	**$9,925,000 –**	**100.00%**

Neither the solicitors nor the IAs have a claim of ownership on the revenue base produced by the clients they brought to the RIA alliance. Passive ownership positions are significant only if the RIA is sold. Passive owners do not participate in the overall profitability of the RIA. Active owners do.

Without the eleven alliances (three solicitors, four IAs, two passive owners, two active owners), the RIA firm's fee revenue would be $4,500,000 instead of $9,925,000, a difference of $5,425,000. If each alliance shared-revenue rate is 15 percent, the net amount paid out to all alliances in shared revenue is $813,750 ($5,425,000 times 15 percent). The balance of $4,611,250 is retained in the RIA and distributed to the active owners (original and alliance) according to the RIA's operating agreement. Assume the operating agreement indicates unassigned revenue net of expenses, or profit, is distributed according to percentage of active ownership only, excluding passive ownership. To determine these percentages, passive owners' revenues are removed from the totals and percentages are recalculated.

Active owners' percentage ownership of their revenue only:

Client revenue of active owner 1	$ 775,000 –	14.52%
Client revenue of active owner 2	$1,025,000 –	19.20%
Client revenue of active owner 3	$2,175,000 –	40.75%
Client revenue of active owner 4	$ 625,000 –	11.71%
CPA firm active owner alliance	$ 529,851 –	9.93%
Benefits group active owner alliance	$ 207,619 –	3.89%
Total percentage ownership, revenue only	$5,337,470 –	100.00%

Assume the RIA's operating expenses are $3,000,000.

Active ownership of unassigned revenues (profit):

Total unassigned revenue (gross profit)	$4,611,250
Operating expenses	$3,000,000
Net profit	**$1,611,250**
Net profit of active owner 1	$233,954 – 14.52%
Net profit of active owner 2	$309,360 – 19.20%
Net profit of active owner 3	$656,584 – 40.75%
Net profit of active owner 4	$188,677 – 11.71%
CPA firm active owner alliance	$159,997 – 9.93%
Benefits group active owner alliance	$ 62,678 – 3.89%

There are alternative methods and percentage calculations of distributing net profit among the active owners, all of which should be detailed in the operating agreement.

Solicitors and IAs in good standing enter the retirement phase when each wants to end the alliance. The total solicitor revenue is $600,000. The total IA revenue is $3,000,000 revenue base. For this analysis, the payout periods from the above summary are used: solicitors receive two months of continued payout for every twelve months in the alliance and IAs receive four months for every twelve.

Solicitor retirement phase buyout:

Solicitor 1 (in alliance for seven years):	$290,000 x 15%= $43,500 per year rate for one year and two months (seven years times two months per year), for a total of $50,750.
Solicitor 2 (in alliance for four years):	$110,000 x 15% = $16,500 per year rate for eight months (four years times two months per year), for a total of $11,000.
Solicitor 3 (in alliance for two years):	$200,000 x 15% = $30,000 per year rate for four months (two years times two months per year), for a total of $10,000.

IA retirement phase buyout:

IA 1 (in alliance for eight years):	$1,400,000 x 15% = $210,000 per year for two years and eight months (eight years times four months per year), for a total of $560,000.
IA 2 (in alliance for seven years):	$610,000 x 15% = $91,500 per year for two years and four months (seven years times four months per year), for a total of $213,500.
IA 3 (in alliance for four years):	$500,000 x 15% = $210,000 per year for one year and four months (four years times four months per year), for a total of $100,000.
IA 4 (in alliance for three years):	$490,000 x 15% = $210,000 per year for one year (three years times four months per year), for a total of $73,500.

Passive owners entering the retirement phase, according to the summaries above, would each receive 50 percent of the total revenue base of the clients they referred to the alliance to be paid out over a period specified in the operating agreement.

Passive ownership buyout:

Passive owner 1:	$800,000 x 50% = $400,000
Passive owner 2:	$350,000 x 50% = $175,000

Active owners do not retire. They are bought out by the RIA firm. According to the summary, active owners receive 75 percent of the total revenue base of the clients they referred to the alliance, also paid out over a period specified in the operating agreement.

Active ownership buyout:

CPA active owner:	$500,000 x 75% = $375,000
Business group active owner:	$175,000 x 75% = $131,250

8 | An Off-the-Shelf Alternative

Honkamp Krueger Financial Services

Investment advisers who are contemplating strategic alliances with CPA firms should take note of this fact: Honkamp Krueger Financial Services (HKFS) is a competitor. CPA firms that want to enter into the financial-services industry and don't want to ally with a local investment adviser might want to turn to the Dubuque, Iowa-based HKFS. HKFS was founded by Honkamp Krueger & Co., a fifty-four-year-old traditional accounting firm, and offers a canned product—a standardized, complete strategic-alliance kit. It is already assembled, tested, and operational. All the CPA firm must do is plug into HKFS's apparatus and the alliance is up and running.

HKFS—The RIA

HKFS markets its services not to the general public but directly to CPA firms that have an interest in offering investment advice and services to its client base. Its processes and procedures are designed specifically for this group.

In order to more fully understand HKFS as an investment adviser, both parts of its Form ADV, a document that leaves nothing to the imagination, are dissected. Then attention is drawn to the elements that are the most relevant to the CPA firm giving consideration to engaging HKFS.

Finally, the methods HKFS uses to bring its services to the CPA profession—marketing, licensing and business structure—are examined.

ADV Part I

Details about HKFS, according to its ADV Part I, revised May 2003, are accessible on the SEC's website (www.adviserinfo.sec.gov/IAPD/Content/IapdMain/iapd_SiteMap.aspx) under SEC # 801-50939 or IARD/CRD # 106237. Those facts are as follows:
—It manages more than $448 million and is therefore registered with and regulated by the SEC
—It is also registered in fourteen states in addition to Iowa (its main office location)
—It is registered as a corporation
—It has between eleven and fifty employees
—It engages between fifty-one and 250 other entities to solicit clients on its behalf, mostly CPA firms
—It has more than 2,000 clients and over 3,100 accounts
—It performs financial-planning services for fewer than ten clients annually
—It does not maintain custody of its clients' securities
—It responded "no" to all twenty-four historical disciplinary disclosure questions, which means it has behaved itself
—It is directly owned by ten individuals; four own 10 percent or more but less than 25 percent; the remaining own at least 5 percent but less than 10 percent; three of the four that own between 10 percent and 25 percent are noncontrolling owners, and the fourth is a controlling owner; all but one of those owning between 5 percent and 10 percent are controlling owners; in total, there are six controlling owners and four noncontrolling owners; it has no indirect owners
—In addition to its main office in Dubuque, Iowa, it maintains four others—Johnston, Iowa; Omaha, Nebraska; St. Louis, Missouri; Madison, Wisconsin; and its website address is www.hkfs.com.

ADV Part II

HKFS is required to provide its ADV Part II to two entities: its regulatory body and prospective clients prior to signing an agreement; it is required to provide it to no one else. However, anyone can request a copy from the SEC or any one of the states in which HKFS is registered. (HKFS was kind enough to provide its most current ADV Part II to the author.)

The facts according to HKFS's ADV Part II, revised June 2004 and available from HKFS upon request:

—Ninety-eight percent of its services are investment supervisory services

—These services are paid for by the client in one of three ways—percentage of assets under management, hourly charges, or fixed fees

—It serves all types of clients except investment companies

—On behalf of its clients, it employs all types of investments except warrants, commodity options, and futures contracts

—Its methods of security analysis include charting, fundamental, technical, and cyclical

—Its main sources of information are financial publications, research prepared by others, corporate rating services, annual reports and other SEC-filed documents, and company press releases

—Its investment strategies include long term, short term, 30-day trading, margin, and options

—It does not require investment advisers registered with it to have a college degree, only to be licensed properly and "have substantial training and experience in financial services"

—It is engaged in the sale of life insurance to a significant degree, noting, "Applicant is licensed as an Iowa insurance agency and derives substantial revenue from insurance sales"

—Some of its employees are registered reps with ProEquities, its broker/dealer

—It engages Schwab Institutional as an "other investment adviser"

—Some owners are part owners of Kidder Benefits, a pension consultant

—It may recommend the client buy or sell securities in which one of its employees might have a financial interest; however HKFS asserts such an occurrence would be "purely coincidental" and would be fully disclosed to the client

—It does not require a minimum dollar amount to open an account

—It reviews client accounts on a schedule agreed to by the investment adviser who is responsible for the account and the client

—It has the authority to determine, without obtaining client consent, securities to be bought and sold, amount of the securities to be bought and sold, the broker or dealer used, and commission rates paid

—It receives additional compensation, ranging from $250 to $10,000 annually, from vendors to assist in paying for annual conferences to train and educate its investment advisers and registered reps; HKFS notes that this could present conflicts of interest

—It receives referrals from various entities with which it maintains solicitor's agreements

Highlights (Detailed in Schedule F, ADV Part II)

Fees

HKFS's fee structure has two levels: discretionary and nondiscretionary. Discretion means HKFS has full authority to make the investment decisions and transactions. Nondiscretionary means HKFS is directed by the account holders and they facilitate transactions through HKFS's custodian.

Discretionary:

Assets under management	Maximum annual fee
Up to $1,000,000	2.75%
$1,000,001–$3,000,000	2.50%
$3,000,001 and up	Negotiable

Nondiscretionary:

Assets under management	Maximum annual fee
Up to $5,000,000	1.00%
$5,000,001–$10,000,000	0.75%
$10,000,001 and up	Negotiable

Note that the fees cited are "maximum annual" fees. All fees are negotiable, and HKFS asserts, "most actual fees are materially below the maximums shown." These fees do not include the expense ratio of mutual funds used by HKFS in its discretionary or nondiscretionary management. Ninety percent of all securities used in the management of HKFS client accounts are mutual funds.

Most RIA ADV Part II forms cite fees that are higher than what is eventually offered to the client, and declare they are negotiable. The specific fees charged to a client are outlined in an RIA's asset management agreement and are normally lower than those stated in the ADV. HKFS is no different.

In general, its total fee charged to a CPA firm's clients is 1.50 percent, again not including the mutual fund expense ratio, an industry average of which is 1.43 percent. HKFS receives 0.70 percent and the CPA firm 0.80 percent. Under normal circumstances, HKFS holds its 0.70 percent constant and requires the CPA firm to adjust downward if the client demands a reduction. However, HKFS says that under some conditions (depending mostly on the size of the CPA firm and its potential) its portion is negotiable.

John R. Darrah, HKFS chief operating officer, provided further insight on HKFS operations. He stated that "our standard agreement is 0.70 percent that we take on up to a $1 million account. Above that, we may negotiate. The total fee to the client depends on several factors as determined by the individual CPA/IAR (investment adviser representatives)—competition, type of account, size of the relationship, et cetera. It is correct that the fund expenses are on top of that."

Asset Management

HKFS's investment committee, consisting of five individuals—two lawyers, two certified financial planners (CFPs), and a chartered financial analyst (CFA)—directs its general asset management decisions. The financial industry regards a CFA, who earns the mark by completing a rigorous, three-phase test administered over three years, as being more professionally qualified than others to render investment direction; she is the committee chair. The committee meets monthly, or when market forces dictate. More than 90 percent of investment positions within client portfolios are accomplished by the purchase of mutual funds within Schwab Institutional accounts.

HKFS predominately uses mutual funds from American, MFS, Schwab, Third Avenue, Wasatch, Franklin Templeton, and William Blair fund families. These mutual funds are either no-load or load-waived, meaning the positions are bought at net asset value (NAV) without sales charge. Thus, there is no commission generated by the purchase of these funds; investor accounts are assessed an annual asset management fee by HKFS. HKFS advises that these fund families can change at any time.

HKFS's ADV does not stipulate the general methodology it uses to guide its clients' investment policy statements, but marketing material provided by the firm indicates that HKFS employs Modern Portfolio Theory (MPT). This theory purports to accomplish diversification in the most efficient manner possible. In fact, the most common term used in dialogue about the MFT is "efficient frontier." An efficient frontier is depicted on an XY graph as an arc, points along which risk and reward are the most compatible. The three most prominent elements of developing an MPT efficient frontier are returns, standard deviation, and correlation coefficients, but can also include such factors as Sharpe ratio, capital asset pricing model, beta, alpha, R-squared, and the like. If HKFS conforms to the fundamental model and uses the elements of returns, standard deviation, and correlation coefficient, it has adopted a tested and reliable method of guiding investment policy. But advisers and CPAs shouldn't assume it does. They should ask the firm to demonstrate how it has constructed an existing client portfolio using MPT.

An exceptional software program offering MPT analysis and portfolio development is Integrated Capital Engine (ICE), available at www.advisoryworld.com.

Financial Planning

If a CPA firm considering a strategic alliance with HKFS believes that financial planning is critical, it might be wise to offer that service in-house. According to item A on Schedule F, 98 percent of HKFS services are investment supervisory in nature and a mere 1 percent involves financial planning. In the ensuing explanation on Schedule F, HKFS states, "Applicant does not hold itself out as performing financial-planning services, but recognizes some aspects of its services may fall under the definition of financial planning."

HKFS has checked item 8C(4) on its Form ADV Part II, indicating it has "arrangements that are material to its advisory business of its clients with a related person who is a financial-planning firm." In the explanation of this point on Schedule F, it notes that the "majority of applicant's stock is owned by partners of a CPA firm. Fee-based financial-planning services may be provided on an incidental basis by these CPA partners." It appears that when HKFS clients express an interest in financial planning, they are directed across the hall to the partners of Honkamp Kruger & Co., P.C. (HK & Co.), a move that might cause a CPA firm considering a strategic alliance with HKFS to be wary.

Despite the technical revelations of the ADV Part II, Darrah explains, "We leave it up to our CPA firms to make the determination as to how financial planning is handled. HK & Co. does financial planning incidental to its CPA business. Many people our CPA firm refers to HKFS have already been through a financial-planning process with the CPA. Other CPA firms may have their own estate-planning or financial-planning service. We would not suggest that their clients use HK & Co. Sometimes, however, the other CPA firms may engage HK & Co. for assistance with the process if the other CPA firm needs backup."

Ownership

CPA firms might want to pay particular attention to HKFS's answer to three assertions: item seven, assertion B; item eight, assertion C(4), and item eight, assertion C(7). The response to these three statements is quite revealing about the origin and makeup of HKFS.

In item seven, "Other Business Activities," assertion B states "Applicant [HKFS] sells products or services other than investment advice to clients." HKFS checked this line, which requires elaboration in Schedule F. There HKFS discloses the following:

"Some of the applicant's employees and associates are licensed to sell life and health insurance products in Iowa and other states. Applicant is licensed as an Iowa insurance agency and derives substantial revenue from insurance sales…some of the owners (of HKFS) are Certified Public Accountants and partners in the firm of Honkamp Krueger & Co., P.C., a public accounting firm." HKFS derives roughly 30 percent of its revenue from the sale of risk products—meaning insurance.

Item eight is "Other Financial Industry Activities or Affiliations." Assertion C inquires whether "Applicant has arrangements that are material to its advisory business or its clients with a related person who is a…" There are several choices for answers. Choice four reads "financial-planning firm." Although HKFS did not check this choice, it does provide an elaboration on Schedule F, which indicates that it should be checked. Schedule F states, "Majority of applicant's stock is owned by partners of a CPA firm. Fee-based financial-planning services may be provided on an incidental basis by these CPA partners." The CPA firm is not identified directly but its identity is implied in that the majority of its partners own HKFS.

Choice seven reads "accounting firm." HKFS checked number seven. In Schedule F, this insight is provided:

Applicant does not render accounting advice nor tax preparation services to its clients. Rather, to the extent that a client requires accounting advice and/or tax preparation services, applicant, if requested, will recommend the services of a certified public accountant, all of which services shall be rendered independent of the applicant pursuant to a separate agreement between the client and the certified public accountant. Specifically, some shareholders of Honkamp Krueger Financial Services, Inc. are also partners of Honkamp Kruger & Co., P.C., a certified public accounting firm. As discussed above, to the extent that Honkamp Krueger & Co., P.C. provides accounting and/or tax preparation services to any clients, including clients of the applicant, all such services shall be performed by Honkamp Kruger & Co., P.C. in its individual professional capacity, independent of the applicant. Many of the applicant's Investment

Advisor Representatives are affiliated with certified public accounting firms. These Investment Advisor Representatives and certified public accounting firms have no affiliation with Honkamp Kruger & Co., P.C.

Item eight, assertion C(4) simply confirms that the majority owners of HKFS are also partners in Honkamp Krueger & Co., P.C. The other two assertions and their explanations are contradictory. HKFS checked B of item seven, which states: "Applicant sells products or services other than investment advice to clients." In this case the services being sold to HKFS clients are accounting and tax preparation. But in the explanation of item eight C(7) above, HKFS declares "Applicant does not render accounting advice nor tax preparation services to its clients."

Which is correct? Either HKFS does sell Honkamp Krueger & Co., P.C. accounting and tax services to its clients, or it doesn't.

The correct answer is, it does...but only if the client requests such services and is within the Dubuque, Iowa, area proper. This conclusion can be drawn from the fact that assertion B of item seven was checked, rather than assertion A.

Assertion A reads, "Applicant is actively engaged in a business other than giving investment advice." This assertion says nothing about selling the products or services of that business to the applicant's clients. This would apply if HKFS, say, owned a copper mining company in Argentina. If HKFS, in fact, does not sell Honkamp Krueger & Co., P.C. accounting services to its clients, it would have checked assertion A, not B, the one that states it does.

However, despite what this acute analysis of its ADV Part II reveals, Darrah maintains the above scenario is parochial. "HKFS does not sell accounting services to any clients on behalf of Honkamp Krueger & Co. Many of Honkamp Krueger & Co. clients are referred to HKFS for investment and risk management services by Honkamp Krueger & Co. If a local area client of HKFS who is not a current client of Honkamp Krueger & Co. asks us about accounting services, we will certainly suggest that they contact Honkamp Krueger & Co. for information. End-user clients outside our Dubuque area are, first, clients of the other CPA firm and that particular CPA firm is providing their accounting services. We do not refer any of those people to Honkamp Krueger & Co."

Because it does sell the services to HKFS clients if the client inquires about such services and is within the general geographic boundaries of Dubuque, Iowa, the SEC requires that it check assertion B. The SEC does not care whether the accounting service is sold before or after an inquiry. If HKFS had checked assertion A and not assertion B, and then responded to an inquiry by an HKFS client regarding accounting and tax service of Honkamp Krueger & Co., P.C., it would be in violation of its own ADV. From a technical reporting standpoint, HKFS is between a rock and a hard place. From a practical standpoint, it will pursue HKFS clients on behalf of Honkamp Krueger & Co., P.C. who inquire about accounting and tax services.

Darrah indicates that referrals back to Honkamp Krueger & Co. from HKFS are confined to the Dubuque area. But this geographic restriction does not preclude HKFS from fulfilling its reporting duty, as it has, of describing in its ADV Schedule F that it does refer clients to Honkamp & Krueger. If HKFS were to identify such a geographic restriction in Schedule F of its ADV, it might allay any competition worries of CPAs it is courting.

HKFS—The Registered Rep Branch Office

The registered reps of HKFS do sell commission products—more from mutual fund sales than from the sales of variable annuities and variable life insurance. This commissioned activity means HKFS is affiliated with a brokerage firm: ProEquities. HKFS's main office in Dubuque, Iowa, acts as the branch office to those CPAs within its system that are registered reps with ProEquities. The RR within the HKFS system receives between 50 percent and 70 percent of the gross dealer concession received from ProEquities.

HKFS—Method of Operation

HKFS markets to two tiers: the CPA firm and the CPA firm's clients. The CPA firms are not the source of revenue for HKFS. Their clients are. Those clients are also the source of revenue for the CPA firms. The message HKFS brings to CPAs is also two-tiered: additional client service and additional revenue.

As Darrah explains it, "One of the things our affiliated CPA firms like about our program is that we understand the CPA culture, since our 'founding stockholders' are CPAs. We understand how they function. Our CPA shareholders are often involved in and instrumental in engaging new CPA affiliates because those prospective CPAs we are engaging like the fact that we have a close relationship to a CPA firm. They do not see it as a competitive situation."

A CPA firm considering engaging HKFS must first decide whether it will receive fees only or fees and commissions. Licensing to accommodate this decision is the first step. Either one CPA or a number of CPAs within the firm will enter the licensing process for either a RR or IA or both.

HKFS currently employs seven field "financial advisers" (FAs). Each is housed in HKFS's four locations through the Midwest.

Darrah regards these individuals as crucial to client service. "The outside FAs are important because they develop deep relationships with the CPAs they work with. Our home office management team maintains frequent contact with the outside CPAs on large case management and compliance, and during two annual conferences we hold for all our CPAs, as well as through visits and calls. We also maintain service assistants in the home office, who provide help for the FAs and CPAs, so our outside CPAs get to know many of us in the home office, and so they understand that systems and processes are driven from here. Those close relationships in the field and our high level of personalized support from the home office to each of our CPA affiliates is the key to building business in those CPA offices."

Each CPA firm that joins the rolls of HKFS is assigned a FA to assist in licensing, marketing, and tending to client service. If a CPA firm is large enough or presents exceptional revenue potential, HKFS will plant a FA inside the offices of the CPA firm to assist in directly integrating the firm's efforts with those of HKFS.

Once a CPA firm decides to engage HKFS and once proper licensing has been established, marketing is the next order of business. The FA and the CPA firm work together to determine the best means of bringing the service to the CPA firm's clients. Most of this effort involves awareness meetings within the halls of the CPA firm; these meetings are aimed at the CPA firm's current client base.

Once a client decides to entrust his or her financial well being to the CPA firm and HKFS, the client, the FA, and the CPA commence a five step process:

1 A review of the client's career and family plans, income needs, personal goals, investment situation, risk tolerance, and tax bracket. These are all sewn up in an Investment Policy Statement (IPS), a fancy industry phrase for how a client's assets are invested. As mentioned, HKFS subscribes to the Modern Portfolio Theory, an analytical method for achieving the greatest possible return at the lowest historical risk.

2 A review of the client's risk exposure: life, disability, long-term care, etc.

3 The implementation of the client decisions. Once the program is in place, HKFS's investment committee monitors and maintains the financial balance of the account.

4 A mutually accepted chronological schedule for revisiting each program is agreed upon among the client, the CPA, and the FA. This could be quarterly, semiannually or annually.

5 Periodically, the client, the CPA, and the FA gather to reassess the client's goals to determine if they continue to match the client's needs. If not, adjustments are made.

HKFS has lost only one CPA firm as a client; the firm choose to operate in a separate investment advisory business model. HKFS has encountered the departure of a few individual CPAs who are IAs or RRs within one of its CPA firm clients. Who "owns" the investment clients that the departing CPA has brought to HKFS? That determination is an open question. According to Darrah, that decision is not in the hands of HKFS. "Our first-line client is the CPA firm, so in the few cases like this that we've been through, we've relied on the internal policies of the CPA firm to determine the status of the clients that particular CPA has added to HKFS over time."

9 | Two Case Studies

FREDRICK "FREDDY" WITHERS, CPA
SOLE PROPRIETOR

HORIZON FINANCIAL ADVISORS, LLC

Fredrick "Freddy" Withers, CPA
Sole Proprietor

Fredrick "Freddy" Withers, with the help of his assistant of twenty-two years, Monica Flowers, practices certified public accountancy from his two-office suite in downtown Minneapolis. Because Monica is efficient and meticulous and because Freddy is creative and knowledgeable, their client base is fiercely loyal. Freddy is that rare bird, even among CPAs: he is genuinely fascinated by the tax code. "To me golf is an incredibly boring sport, so I spend most of my summer studying tax law so I can find holes in it," Freddy says. When clients would ask him for investment advice, Freddy would hand over a list of four or five names of investment advisers and counsel them to interview a few and pick the one they perceived to be the best.

Invariably these clients would rarely investigate these advisers and the following year, at tax time, they would repeat their plea for investment advice from their trusted CPA. Freddy knew they needed

---

Note: Names and cities have been changed to protect the identities of the entities.

investment help and realized that they would not pursue outside professionals; they wanted his guidance.

Acknowledging this reality, Freddy became a registered representative with the independent brokerage firm Raymond James. Freddy spent the summer of 1997, after the crucible of tax time, studying for and passing the requisite tests: Series 7 (to give advice and sell securities) and Series 24 (to act as the compliance officer of his little branch office).

Independent brokerage firms do not normally allow an individual with little or no production (sales) track record to establish an autonomous office. Typically such novices are required to become satellite offices of an existing branch office, whose Series 24 acts as that satellite's compliance officer and also expects a cut of all the novice's commissions. Freddy would have none of this; undergoing external corporate control was fundamentally at odds with his personality. Assisted by two dozen letters penned by those clients who repeatedly begged for his advice, Freddy persuaded Raymond James he would rapidly grow his practice to the minimum commission level to justify his own office. For this concession, Freddy agreed to quarterly compliance audits by Raymond James' regional vice president for the first year of operation. Raymond James felt a bit nervous about an inexperienced Series 24 overseeing a branch office, especially his own office exclusively. In effect, Freddy would be monitoring himself; an activity that would cause any compliance officer to suffer shortness of breath.

Freddy spent late summer and most of fall of 1997 putting in place the operational structure to accommodate investment business. He decided not to hire an investment-related assistant until one was needed, relying initially on Monica's thorough and precise character to execute the details of the new undertaking. Monica, with whom Freddy shared profits, was apprehensive and less than thrilled. "That's her nature," Freddy explained, and then added "but I probably should have listened to her."

Before breathing a word of his new service to his clients:

♦ Three additional file cabinets were stuffed into Monica's office; in them the customary battery of client and compliance forms, compliance files, prospectuses, and fresh files for those clients Freddy already knew were his.

♦ A separate desk was wedged next to Monica's normal desk (upon her demand), where she could segregate the preparation and control of the massive flow of investment paperwork from that of the equally substantial flow of tax paperwork.

♦ A marker board was hung on the back of the door connecting Monica's and Freddy's office; it was used to track the status of client paperwork, compliance and noncompliance, as it moved through the office process.

Monica studied for and passed the Series 11 test, authorizing her to execute client trades upon Freddy's cue. Monica was becoming more nervous by the day.

Because Freddy's present computer had minimal hard drive space left, an additional computer system was purchased and tucked under the new desk; it housed all the software needed to conduct securities business through Raymond James.

Freddy and Monica spent three days at Raymond James's headquarters in St. Petersburg, Florida, training on the new software, the main component of which gave Monica and Freddy the ability to execute trades by a few keystrokes.

Then they unveiled their investment adviser business.

Three years later, in the summer of 2000, Freddy finally came to regret his decision to unilaterally offer investment advice. "All the behavior and activity necessary to conduct securities business properly, efficiently, and profitably was a nightmare," he explained. What Freddy did not anticipate was that most of the primary CPA clients he translated into investment clients began vigorously referring other investors to Freddy, most of whom were too small to be profitable and none of whom Freddy could decline without alienating the referrers, his precious CPA clients. Poor Monica, occasionally weeping and frantically managing two gorged pipelines of paperwork, demanded relief.

Had Freddy not hired a full-time and a part-time employee, he would have lost Monica, lost control of the investment practice, and severely wounded his CPA practice. "Not only are the operational aspects of compliance and process and procedures a huge burden, but the product wholesalers who want to waste my time at lunch pitching their products literally oozed out of the woodwork. I just didn't have time to do all this and to keep my accounting practice razor sharp."

During the three years as a part-time investment adviser, Freddie had closely acquainted himself with Sharon Lacker, a full-time investment adviser whose office was a few blocks away in downtown Minneapolis. During the final few months of coming to grips with the certain demise of his investment advisory business Freddy confided in Sharon about his growing sense of despair.

During the course of their many conversations in the summer of 2000, it became apparent that the office leases for both Sharon and Freddy were terminating within just twenty days of each other that September. The opportunity to combine forces had presented itself and within six weeks, Sharon and Freddy had agreed to share office space and clients. (Although each office had two adjoining mutual doors, each entity maintained a separate entrance from the public hallway.)

Freddy relinquished his and Monica's direct role in the process of gaining investment clients (to Monica's relief). All clients were now directed to Sharon across the hall, who was well equipped to engage them properly and professionally. Occasionally, Freddy would attend initial meetings and would help in maintaining client happiness. Freddy transferred his RR brokerage affiliation to that of Sharon's, and Sharon handed over 60 percent of all commissions and fees to Freddy on revenue generated by the clients he sent to her.

Freddy and Monica were pleased with the new arrangement. Both returned to bringing impeccable accounting services to their clients while earning 60 percent on all investment revenue for merely pointing the clients to the office doors they and Sharon shared. It's hard to think of a happier ending for all involved.

Horizon Financial Advisors, LLC

In 1998, Roger Turrgle left Winslow, Masters and Turrgle, a financial advisory firm in Seattle, to join with Hollis & Turner, CPAs, also of Seattle, in a new RIA firm they dubbed Horizon Financial Advisors (HFA). Turrgle, after accumulating more than eighteen years in the investment advisory profession, had concluded early in 1998 that aligning with a CPA firm in some fashion was a solid business decision, both from a client service perspective and from a profitability perspective.

Prior to deciding on Hollis & Turner, Turrgle spent six months interviewing four other CPA firms in Seattle. His goal was to discover a firm that would push beyond the mere motion of passing clients back and forth for compensation. He sought an integrated and binding business relationship because he felt such solidity was better for his clients. The arrangement would also foster his clients' trust and thus lead to high-quality referrals.

Hollis & Turner was the only CPA firm that understood that establishing a separate entity (i.e., HFA) was the ideal way of building an enduring relationship with an investment adviser. HFA evolved through two stages: initial and revised.

The initial operating agreement for HFA split ownership equally among Turrgle and the three partners of Hollis & Turner, each owning a fixed 25 percent. At the close of each quarter all net revenue was distributed according to ownership. The notion from the outset was that each owner would be an active and equal participant in the addition of client assets and that ultimately, over time, revenue distributions would reach parity.

This phase lasted only five quarters. The revised phase was incorporated for two reasons: 1) the concept of equality did not play out as anticipated, causing a number of heated debates and 2) a very successful, high profile investment adviser in the Seattle area, John Stearns, wanted to join HFA as an owner, a move not accommodated by the

Note: Names and cities have been changed to protect the identities of the entities.

initial operating agreement. Share dilution was discussed, but it was decided that the initial model was not functioning properly and that the timing of Stearns' request to join HFA was perfect for fixing the ownership issue.

Turrgle introduced the concept of asset-based ownership in an RIA and the three partners of Hollis & Turner fully understood it, realizing that an ownership position should be equal to the amount of business brought to the RIA by each owner. Furthermore, Stearns let it be known that asset-based ownership would be the only structure he would accept; he was a performer and wanted to be compensated for it.

Asset-based ownership became the core of the revised operating agreement, which also stipulated that each owner would receive a minimum of 30 percent of the revenue generated by assets brought to HFA by that owner. (Through research it was determined that HFA would maintain the benchmark of 38 percent of revenue being consumed by operational expenses, leaving a 32 percent profit margin, net of the 30 percent individual payout.)

The revised HFA started with each owner writing a $15,000 check to HFA, which was recorded on HFA's balance sheet as long-term debt.

Two weeks later, Samuel Hollis brought in the new HFA's first client—a widow's portfolio of over $5 million, netting $41,250 of HFA annual revenue; at that moment Hollis owned 100 percent of HFA. Three days later Turrgle added two clients, one bringing $3 million and the second $4.5 million, netting $65,100 of HFA annual revenue, catapulting him past Hollis in HFA ownership. A week later, Stearns brought his friend's $2.5 million retirement funds to HFA, generating $24,500 of annual revenue.

At the end of the first month of operation HFA ownership looked like this:

	Annual Revenue	Percent of Ownership	Personal Revenue
Turrgle	$ 65,100	49.75%	$19,530
Hollis	$ 41,250	31.52%	$12,375
Stearns	$ 24,500	18.72%	$ 7,350
Turner	$0	0%	$ 0
Carter	$0	0%	$ 0
Total	$130,850	100.00%	$39,255

Alarmed, Mark Turner and Sarah Carter sprang into action. By the end of the first quarter the picture had changed:

	Annual Revenue	Percent of Ownership	Personal Revenue
Stearns	$165,100	25.93%	$ 49,530
Hollis	$145,000	22.78%	$ 43,500
Turrgle	$137,500	21.61%	$ 41,250
Carter	$101,500	15.94%	$ 30,450
Turner	$ 87,500	13.74%	$ 26,250
Total	$636,600	100.00%	$190,980

During the first quarter HFA did not, as hoped, maintain a 38 percent expense overhead. It consumed 41.5 percent of the $636,600 of revenue, leaving a net profit of $181,431 after the distribution of personal revenue from each owner's asset base. It was decided to distribute this profit to the owners according to the provisions in the operating agreement; each owner's portion would be equal to the percent of ownership at the close of the quarter:

	Percent of Ownership	Personal Revenue	Distributed Net Profit	Total Income
Stearns	25.93%	$ 49,530	$ 47,045	$ 96,575
Hollis	22.78%	$ 43,500	$ 41,330	$ 84,830
Turrgle	21.61%	$ 41,250	$ 39,207	$ 80,457
Carter	15.94%	$ 30,450	$ 28,920	$ 59,370
Turner	13.74%	$ 26,250	$ 24,929	$ 51,179
Total	100.00%	$190,980	$181,431	$372,411

As HFA gained numerous quarters of experience under its revised organizational structure, the partners noticed on occasion that when an owner added a substantial amount of revenue to the total revenue late in a quarter, it increased that owner's relative position enough to trigger some debate about the validity of working on absolutes. According to Turrgle, the problem was quickly fixed. "A few quarters into the new agreement, we started calculating ownership by using the average of the quarter's beginning revenue position and its ending revenue position for each one of us," Turrgle explained. "This helped to some degree to smooth out late-quarter spikes."

In a theoretical sense, all factors remaining flat throughout a quarter, if each owner had been operating as an independent RIA and were able to hold the same expense ratio of 41.5 percent, creating a net payout of 58.5 percent on only the revenue each brought in, his total personal revenue would be precisely the same as that which he received as an owner of HFA. So in that comparative sense, there is no advantage from a revenue perspective in sharing net profit. Thus, setting the immediate revenue payout, in HFA's case at a minimum of 30 percent, is arbitrary.

Incoming revenues at HFA never remained flat, rendering theory irrelevant. Therein lies the strength of this model, at least from a revenue standpoint: the motivation generated by the activity of the each owner on the other owners is compelling. Even if only one of the owners is energetic and funneling client assets into HFA, the others are forced to respond in order to keep pace.

From a balance sheet value perspective, ownership positions have greater meaning and substance. Unlike commissions, fee-based revenue is continuous and therefore carries value and is saleable. Its proportionate effect is identical to that of share revenue. If the HFA is sold, each owner's share of the sale proceeds is identical to the assets that owner historically delivered to HFA.

The addition of Stearns also triggered the decision of the owners to register Horizon Securities (HS) with the NASD as an introducing brokerage firm. (In the securities business, an "introducing firm" is one that typically employs individual brokers who take customer orders and see they are executed. A firm registered as a "clearing firm" holds the customer's cash and securities and produces statements describing assets it holds on deposit for the customer. Many smaller firms register as introducing firms because the capital requirements are less than for clearing firms.) Turrgle was an RR affiliated with the independent brokerage firm Linsco Private Ledger when HFA was formed, and he continued to push commission-based investments through it, although at a trickle, and from which he received 12(b)1 proceeds. Stearns, on the other hand, was affiliated with Royal Alliance, another independent brokerage firm. Because the NASD forbids RRs of two different brokerage firms to share the same address, one of the firms had to be fired and all clients moved to the other firm, a long and agonizing ordeal.

Initially, Turrgle claimed HFA seniority and informed Stearns that he would have to transfer his 275 clients from Royal Alliance to Linsco Private Ledger. After numerous discussions it was decided that the five owners would create their own brokerage firm and both Turrgle and Stearns would transfer all clients from their respective brokerage firms into the new one. Stearns elaborated on the rationale for creating their own brokerage firm. "We saved the 10 percent haircut that Roger (Turrgle) and I were taking from our broker/dealers; his was LPL and mine was Royal. We figured the combined annual savings in revenue would overcome the cost of establishing the brokerage firm within four years." Both Turrgle and Stearns would hire a shared part-time assistant to administer the transfer of clients.

Becoming a brokerage firm later proved to be even more fortuitous. "Ten months after launching the Horizon Securities, and after having shifted all our clients to it, Frontier Bank & Trust, a local bank here in the Seattle area, probed us about HS providing investment and financial planning services to its customers," Turrgle explained. Frontier had twelve branches peppered throughout the Seattle area and wanted HS to train a specific bank employee at each branch in selling investments. Each employee would become a dual employee: hired and managed daily by the bank and licensed and affiliated with HS, which would be responsible for all investment compliance issues. Each bank location would become a branch office of HS.

At the outset, HFA owners were chilly to the idea. Because most of the activity generated by bank customers would fall below HFA's minimum of $250,000, nearly all the sales and transaction activity would flow through HS, which would most assuredly become an administrative quagmire. The intent of creating HS was not to mass-produce hundreds of commissionable accounts but to privately house commissioned assets of the owners' clients and the clients of any other potential RR associates added to HS later. (At the time Frontier approached HS, two RRs were in negotiations to affiliate with HS.)

But a pro forma was constructed demonstrating that the HS/Frontier alliance could generate over a half a million dollars in revenue for HS (at a 60 percent HS/40 percent Frontier split) in the first three years, even with performance variables held to a minimum: if each Frontier branch produced three customers per month at $11,500 of investable assets per customer and increased that production by a 2.5 percent annual rate. (Preliminary research indicated that the $11,500 mark was the average investment per customer arriving through bank doors.) In addition, the alliance would expose HFA, the RIA, to Frontier's high-net-worth clients, those above the $250,000 floor. In addition, the Hollis & Turner CPA firm would be exposed to these same high-net-worth individuals as well as the bank's business customers. All these profitability avenues changed their minds about the HS/Frontier venture.

The HFA partners took the next step and launched extensive due diligence by interviewing a number of investment advisory sources in other parts of the country that had engaged banks and other savings institutions and discovered that indeed the venture was profitable. "However, every contact expressed the identical misgiving," said Turrgle. "They said that eventually bank management will decide to create their own brokerage firm and replicate all HS's responsibilities in our deal and cut HS out of the profit loop."

To help alleviate this possibility, the partners of HS decided to offer Frontier Bank a 40 percent ownership stake in HS itself, cal-culating that such a move would help deter any future attempts at carving HS from the picture. The bank was not offered the same for HFA. The partners recognized there was less loss of value in forfeiting a portion of ownership in HS because its revenue source was commission, which is not a perpetual and somewhat dependable stream and therefore holds less value than the fee-based revenue stream of HFA. The alliance commenced in early 2001. "Training and licensing took longer than we thought, but once all the reps were in place at each bank branch the sales eventually met our expectations," Turrgle said.

During the period of installing HS into the banks, HFA registered two individual investment advisers to its RIA.

Business proceeded normally for HFA and HS until the summer of 2004 when HFA was approached by Saggert Consulting Company about being acquired. Saggert offered small businesses a full spectrum of employee benefits, including products, services, and consultation. All parties believed the potential acquisition was a good fit with HFA and HS. At the time of this writing, negotiations were still under way. However, it appeared that Spencer Saggert, the consulting company's principal, would become one of the partners in a new umbrella entity that was being considered to house Horizon Financial Advisors, Horizon Securities, and now Horizon Employee Benefits. The name of the umbrella entity is tentatively The Horizon Group.

From a simple four-person alliance to a thriving, diverse, and profitable business that kept opening more and more doors, Horizon's flexible organizational structure has assured its prosperity.

APPENDIX: *Sample Forms and Contracts*

DISCLAIMER: *The forms, contracts, and documents presented here are provided for informational purposes only. These materials and information are not a substitute for obtaining legal advice from the reader's own attorney in the appropriate jurisdiction or state. Proper legal counsel can provide advice that fits the reader's particular facts and the circumstances appropriate to each situation.*

Strategic Alliance Summaries

Solicitor's Agreement

Ownership of Revenue Stream:	No
Revenue-Sharing Rate:	10% on eligible referral revenues from $0 to $50,000
	15% on eligible referral revenues of $50,001 and up
Tax Reporting:	Form 1099
RIA Employee:	No
Approval:	Majority vote of active partners
Retirement Trigger:	Absence of qualified referrals within a one-year period
Retirement Payout Period:	Full revenue stream for two months for every twelve months as solicitor
Regulatory Requirements:	Solicitor's Agreement (includes a Noncompete clause)
	Client Disclosure Statement

Investment Adviser

Ownership of Revenue Stream:	No
Ownership of Booked Clients:	No
Noncompete Agreement:	Yes
Revenue-Sharing Rate:	15% on eligible referral revenues
RIA Employee:	No
Voting Rights:	None
Tax Reporting:	Form 1099
Approval:	Majority vote of active partners
Retirement Trigger:	Majority vote of partners and absence of referrals within a one-year period

Retirement Payout Period:	Full revenue stream for four months for every twelve months as an investment adviser
Regulatory Requirements:	Investment adviser has a spotless U-4
	Investment adviser passes Series 65 exam
	Disclosure in Form ADV Part II, which is provided to clients

Passive Partnership

Ownership of Revenue Stream:	Yes
Capital Contribution:	$5,000
Class B Shares Owned:	5,000
Class A shares Owned:	One share per one dollar of assets referred and under management
Revenue-Sharing Rate:	15% on eligible referral revenues
RIA Financial Reporting:	Balance sheet and projected profit provided
Noncompete Agreement:	Yes
RIA Employee:	No
Voting Rights:	None
Legalities:	Documentation signed outlining all provisions
Tax Reporting:	Partnership K-1
Approval:	Majority vote of active partners
Retirement Trigger:	At request of passive partner
Retirement Payout Period:	Full revenue stream for seven years (continued to estate upon death)
Retirement Buyout Class A:	RIA buys Class B shares for $1 per share
Retirement Buyout Class B:	One year's worth of referred assets, paid out over seven years
Regulatory Requirements:	Disclosure in Form ADV Part I, which is not provided to clients

All terms applicable on "qualified clients" (clients with a minimum of $2,500 in eligible annual revenues, subject to change).

Solicitor's Agreement

Purpose

The purpose of this agreement is to meet requirements set forth by the Investment Advisers Act of 1940 for written agreements between SEC-registered Investment Advisory firms and those persons receiving compensation from them.

Appointment

CPA Inc. (CPA) is appointed an Associate for RIA Inc. (RIA). The scope and limitations of your authority are defined in the following paragraphs. As an Associate, you have only such authority as is specifically given to you by this agreement or by us.

Authority

Under this appointment, you may distribute literature describing our firm and its services; assist in the completion of applications, questionnaires, and related documents; *introduce* new clients to our firm; and accompany clients you have *introduced* when they meet with one of our Investment Counselors.

While this agreement is subject to such rules and regulations as we may deem appropriate and establish from time to time for the efficient administration of this agreement and of our business, it is the intent of this agreement that you be an independent contractor, with full freedom to determine, within the scope of this agreement, the persons with whom you engage in these activities and the method, time, and place of your performance. Accordingly, nothing in this agreement, or any rule or regulation established by us shall create, or be interpreted to create, the relationship of employee and employer between us.

Prohibited Activities

You are specifically **prohibited** from rendering investment advice to any individual or entity on our behalf. Only registered and licensed Investment Counselors, meeting regulatory qualifications and employed by us, may render investment advice on our behalf.

This agreement is personal to you and is, therefore, not transferable. Moreover, no compensation of any kind earned, or to be earned, under this contract may be assigned or pledged without our consent.

Compensation

We agree to compensate you at your customary rate for time billed to us in the performance of authorized activities, subject to the following restrictions, conditions, and limitations:

[a] The invoice must identify and relate to a specific client served;

[b] You must have properly *introduced* the clients by providing them with copies of both our firm's disclosure document (Form ADV Part II) and a written statement disclosing your relationship with us. An acknowledgment of receipt of both, signed and dated by the clients prior to their contract for our services, must be on file with us;

[c] Compensation related to the initial establishment of an account for the identified client may not exceed an amount equal to _____ % of the Counseling Fee we have received from the identified client;

[d] Annual compensation (other than that described at [c]) related to the identified client may not exceed an amount equal to _____ % of the annual Advisory Fees we have received from the identified client;

[e] No compensation shall be deemed to have been earned until we have actually received those fees from the identified client upon which your compensation is being based.

Compliance

[a] Solicitor agrees that it shall perform its duties under this Agreement in a manner consistent with the provisions of the Investment Advisers Act of 1940 ("Act") and other applicable law. Each Customer shall receive, at the time of any solicitation activities, a copy of Adviser's written disclosure statement required by Rule 204-3 of the Act and a separate written disclosure document described in Rule 206(4)-3(b) of the Act, a copy of which is attached as Exhibit A. The parties will obtain a signed statement from each Customer acknowledging receipt of such disclosure statement and document, and the Adviser shall retain a copy thereof as required by Rule 206(4)-3.

[b] Solicitor is not currently a party to any contract or agreement that would prevent or restrict the activities of Solicitor under this Agreement. Solicitor represents that it is not a person described in subparagraphs (A) through (D), inclusive, of Rule 206(4)-3(a)(1)(ii) under the Act.

[c] Solicitor will not pay a fee to any other party in connection with its activities hereunder.

Marketing Materials

Solicitor will utilize only marketing materials supplied or approved by Adviser. Solicitor will not use any sales literature or other materials describing the Adviser or its services without Adviser's prior written approval.

Confidentiality

The parties agree that the materials provided to each other under this Agreement are proprietary in nature and further agree not to disclose or distribute these materials to any party other than as contemplated by this Agreement, unless required by appropriate judicial or regulatory authority. Upon termination of this Agreement, each party will promptly return to the other party all materials provided by such other party in connection with this Agreement.

Termination

The laws applicable to an agency relationship provide that the agency may continue only so long as both of us desire to maintain it. Therefore, this contract may be terminated by either you or us at any time by notice delivered to the other party at the respective addresses shown below.

This agreement will take effect upon acceptance by both parties below.

I have carefully read the foregoing and hereby accept this agreement.

Signed and accepted on _____.

Signed and accepted on _____.

Officer of firm
CPA, Inc. (CPA)
Address

Solicitor's Disclosure Letter

Solicitor's Disclosure Document and Client Acknowledgment Pursuant to Rule 206(4)-3 under the Investment Advisers Act of 1940

Name of Adviser:	Registered Investment Adviser (RIA)
Address of Adviser:	14 South Main, Main, MA 01222
Telephone:	123-966-0033
Name of Solicitor:	CPA, Inc. (CPA)

The above-named Solicitor has entered into an agreement with RIA, a registered investment adviser under the Investment Advisers Act of 1940, under which Solicitor has agreed to solicit clients on behalf of the Adviser. The Adviser has agreed to compensate the Solicitor in an amount equal to [ ] of the fees paid to the Adviser by clients solicited by the Solicitor.

The fees payable by client to the Adviser are the fees stated in Adviser's standard form of client agreement. No additional fees are charged to the client, and there is no fee rate differential to clients because of the compensation paid by the Adviser to the Solicitor.

The Adviser and the Solicitor have agreed to make available to the Solicitor's customers the Adviser's asset allocation services, as well as various mutual fund products administered by the Adviser and distributed by its affiliate. The Adviser and Solicitor are not affiliated.

The undersigned hereby acknowledges receipt of this disclosure document and the Adviser's disclosure statement and acknowledges that he/she has read and understood the information contained therein.

_____   _____
Signature   Date

_____   _____
Signature   Date

Passive Partner Agreement

RIA Inc. (RIA), an investment adviser registered with the Securities and Exchange Commission (SEC), has agreed to add CPA Inc. (CPA) as a passive, noncontrolling partner of RIA Inc. under the following:

Definitions & Conditions

Passive, Noncontrolling Partner: CPA becomes a passive partner of RIA; CPA has no voting rights, is not involved in the daily activities of RIA, and meets the Securities & Exchange Commission's definition of Noncontrolling.

Qualified Referral: a potential client whose investable assets are over RIA's stated minimum, currently $250,000 and subject to change.

Revenue-Sharing Base: annual management fees of those Qualified Referrals introduced to RIA by CPA who become RIA clients.

Revenue-Sharing Rate: 15%

Shared Revenues: Revenue Base times Revenue Rate, paid quarterly, after receipt of Revenue Base from clients referred to RIA by CPA.

Class A Shares: a share class issued by RIA to CPA, one share of which is equal to one dollar, a value that will neither increase nor decrease; CPA will be issued 5,000 shares of Class B Shares in exchange for $5,000.

Retirement Phase: a condition RIA's active partners impose on CPA by majority vote after a period of twelve months during which no Qualified Referrals have been introduced to RIA by CPA; if the Retirement Phase is invoked, CPA has forty-five days to appeal the vote to the partners.

Ownership of Revenue: under the following conditions, CPA owns the Revenue-Sharing Base of those individuals referred to RIA by CPA who become RIA clients:

◆ CPA shall receive the Shared Revenue.

◆ CPA shall receive, upon entering the Retirement Phase, seven years of continued 100% of Shared Revenues; at the end of the seventh year all Shared Revenues and Ownership of the Revenue Base generating the Shared Revenues ends, and all Class B Shares are repurchased from CPA on that final day by RIA.

◆ In the event of CPA's death prior to her entering the Retirement Phase, her estate (or heirs) will receive seven years of continued 100% of Shared Revenues; at the end of the seventh year all Shared Revenues and Ownership of the Revenue Base generating the Shared Revenues ends, and all Class B Shares are repurchased from CPA's estate (or heirs) on that final day by RIA.

◆ In the event of CPA's death after entering the Retirement Phase but before the seventh year of continued 100% of Shared Revenues, her estate (or heirs) will receive the balance of years to be paid out by the identical schedule, at the end of which all Class B Shares are repurchased from CPA's estate (or heirs) by RIA.

◆ In the event RIA is sold prior to CPA entering the Retirement Phase, CPA will receive her portion of the sale proceeds equal to CPA's Revenue-Sharing Base divided by the total Revenue Base sold, and all Class B Shares will be repurchased from CPA by RIA.

◆ In the event RIA is sold after CPA enters the Retirement Phase, the new owners will be given two options: 1) continue the Shared Revenue through the remaining years of the Retirement Phase, or 2) purchase the Shared Revenue outright as negotiated by CPA and the new owners.

◆ All Shared Revenue payouts cease if CPA violates the noncompete clause of this agreement.

Noncompete: CPA agrees not to compete with RIA for the clients CPA has referred to RIA as a Passive Partner for three years after the day the Retirement Phase ends by:

◆ Becoming licensed with the NASD
◆ Registering as an Investment Adviser with another RIA
◆ Registering herself or an entity she creates as a partner or owner in an RIA
◆ Becoming a partner or owner with an existing RIA
◆ Entering into a Solicitor's Agreement with an existing RIA

Approval Method: majority vote of RIA active partners

Employment: CPA will not be employed by RIA.

Nonqualified Referral: if RIA accepts a referral from CPA that is nonqualified and produces commission through the RIA's broker dealer, CPA understands she is not licensed with the NASD and cannot share in this commission; if RIA accepts a referral from CPA that is nonqualified and produces a Revenue-Sharing Base below $1,000 through RIA, CPA understands that RIA will not pay, or accumulate to pay, Shared Revenues below $150 per year (or Revenue-Sharing Rate of 15% times $1,000).

_____   _____

RIA Partner   CPA

_____   _____

Date   Date

RIA Policies & Procedures

Brokerage Usage—Trade Inc. (TI)

RIA has engaged Trade Inc (TI) as its brokerage for trading and as custodian for the securities of RIA's clients. TI is a division of TI, the online investment corporation, traded on the Nasdaq under the symbol TII. All trades (buys and sells) of securities for RIA's clients will be placed through TI. All trades will be placed online. If such service is disrupted, trades will be placed by telephone. The current cost of an online transaction is a flat $10.99. This means that a buy and a sell, commonly referred to as a "round-trip," costs $21.98. The current cost of trades placed by telephone is $24.99 per transaction, or $49.98 for a round-trip. TI provides RIA with a comprehensive Web-based platform through which RIA manages and monitors its clients' assets and portfolios.

Custody of Client Assets

RIA does not retain custody of its clients' assets. The state of _____ prohibits such practice. TI, which acts as custodian on behalf of RIA and its clients, holds all RIA client assets and securities. When a person or entity engages RIA's service and maintains assets at another financial institution, those assets are automatically transferred into an account opened at TI for the new client. Those assets may or may not be liquidated at the previous financial institution prior to their transfer.

Money Flows

RIA prefers wire transfers of cash into a client's existing account. This practice is swifter and more easily tracked and managed. RIA has developed a means that simplifies wire transfers. However, if a client desires (or cannot execute a wire transfer), a personal check can be sent to RIA's place of business (address). RIA will, within forty-eight hours, forward the check to TI for deposit into the client's account.

Reporting (TI & RIA)

TI e-mails monthly brokerage statements directly to RIA's clients. These statements are identical (with regards to information provided) to statements clients are accustomed to receiving from other financial institutions. These statements include: a summary of portfolio valuations for current month and previous month, valuation of each position at the close of the reported month, and transaction activity within the account for the reported month. TI also e-mails trade confirmations to RIA's clients. RIA provides quarterly performance reports for its clients' portfolios. These reports are sent to the client via e-mail. RIA e-mails quarterly management fee invoices to its clients, which it also submits electronically to TI. TI, upon receipt of such invoices, debits each RIA client account in the amount of each invoice. Whenever possible all RIA reporting is via e-mail unless a client cannot or will not accept e-mails.

Trade Allocations

RIA manages three separate portfolios called the ABC Models™. Based on a Financial Plan or a Suitability Profile, a client's assets are placed in one of these three portfolios. Each client's assets are maintained in a separately owned account. They are not commingled. Transactions are often executed for more than one portfolio and for more than one client. Whenever possible, such transaction are "bunched." This means that shares of all clients will be summed and a purchase will be made for the entire "bunch" at the same transaction price. In this fashion, each client receives the same price for the transaction. Roughly 90% of all transactions will be "bunched." When it is not possible to "bunch" transactions, trades will be made randomly among clients.

Personal Trading

RIA's Principal and Investment Advisers participate in the ABC Model portfolios. In instances when the accounts of these RIA individuals require transactions similar to transactions for RIA's client accounts, the transactions of these RIA individuals will be included in "bunch" transactions. In the event that "bunch" transactions cannot be employed, when securities are bought, the positions of the RIA individuals will be purchased after those of all RIA's clients. When securities are sold, the positions of the RIA individuals will be sold after all RIA's client positions are sold. This sequence helps ensure that, under normal market conditions, the accounts of RIA's clients receive a more favorable price than the accounts of RIA individuals.

Referral Arrangements

RIA engages other professional entities via Solicitor's Agreements to refer clients to RIA. Terms of the Solicitor's Agreement provide the other professional entities with compensation for the referrals. RIA's referral agreement is in compliance with the federal regulations as set out in 17 CFR Section 275-206(4)-3, and in each state where state law requires. Each client is given a copy of the referral agreement prior to or at the time of entering into any Advisory contract.

Emergency Business Replication

All operational and investment functions enabled at RIA's primary place of business have been replicated in their entirety at RIA Principal's personal residence.

ABC Models

The methods and securities selections are proprietary to RIA and cannot be shared with entities that are not RIA clients for the purposes of replication. The phrase "ABC Models" is trademarked.

Brochure ADV, Part II

Introduction

The Form ADV Part II is a document filed with the Securities & Exchange Commission (SEC). It is a full-disclosure document providing all the pertinent details of how a Registered Investment Adviser (RIA) establishes, operates, and maintains its relationship with its clients. You can contact the SEC's Investor Assistance and Complaints department to check the veracity of any Registered Investment Adviser registered with them at (202-942-7040) or log on to their Internet site at www.sec.gov. A copy of the ADV is provided to potential clients before engagement. The ADV is offered to existing clients annually. Existing clients can decline or accept to receive it. The ADV provided to potential clients and existing clients can be presented in one of two fashions: 1) a copy of the originally filed document or 2) a brochure version of the originally filed document. The version you're about to read is the Brochure Version. If you wish to receive a copy of the originally filed document, please ask.

Content

I

Eighty percent of RIA's revenue is generated from assets under management (AUM) fees, which are charged as a percentage of AUM. The following is a description of the method of managing assets and the fee structure employed.

> The ABC Model portfolio management style is proprietary to RIA; the term ABC Model is trademarked.

The client's participation in the ABC Model portfolios may or may not be based on the findings of a Financial Plan. If it is mutually agreed by the client and RIA that a Financial Plan (in modular or in whole) is necessary, one will be written and an ABC Model portfolio will be selected based on the Plan findings.

If it is mutually agreed that a Financial Plan (in modular or in whole) is not necessary, an ABC Model portfolio will be selected based on the client's Suitability Profile, a standard industry measure that includes investment objective, risk tolerance, age, income, liquid assets, net worth, and tax bracket.

There are three ABC Model portfolios **with discretionary status**: Dynamic (D), Moderate (M), and Conservative (C). There are two components of each portfolio: Strategic and Tactical.

Strategic: The Strategic component of each ABC Model portfolio consists of three core elements:
1) Individual "Blue Chip" equity securities representing S&P's ten sectors: Energy, Materials, Industrials, Consumer Discretionary, Consumer Cyclicals, Health Care, Financials, Information Technology, Communications, Utilities. Only the percentage distribution among sectors changes from portfolio to portfolio. Not all sectors are represented in all portfolios. These equity positions are monitored on a regular basis and changed infrequently.
2) Individual bonds.
3) Cash.

The percentage distribution among these three elements changes among portfolios.

Tactical: Equities representing specific/various S&P subsectors are periodically bought and sold based on technical and fundamental indicators. Participation in the Tactical component can be declined. **There is no guarantee that the Tactical component will increase the value of any ABC Model portfolio. It is recognized and acknowledged that the Tactical component carries potentially greater risk than the Strategic component of the ABC Model portfolios.**

The Tactical component of the ABC Model methodology is also available as a "stand-alone" Investment Policy Statement.

Transactions and custodial services for the ABC Model portfolio equities are provided by TI.

Clients will receive quarterly performance reports containing the performances for various periods of both the total portfolio and the individual equities within the portfolio.

An annual portfolio review will be offered to the client. The review will include an examination of diversification shifts, risk tolerance shifts, political and economic conditions,
and asset performance relative to market and business cycles. The client and the RIA will
agree on changes (if any) in the portfolio only after considering the tax consequences
of such changes. The facts and findings of the Financial Plan (if one was written) or the
Suitability Profile will be considered as well. Depending upon tax ramifications, the rebalancing of the client's Portfolio is at the mutual discretion of the client and RIA.

Fee Structure

The ABC Model is provided on a fee basis. The client agrees to pay a management fee
based on the total value of the equities in the ABC Model. The fee is stated as an annual
rate in the tables below. The annual rate will be withdrawn quarterly from the client's ABC
Model portfolio (one-fourth the annual rate), one calendar quarter in advance. This with-
drawal will be based on the total market value of the equities in the ABC Model at the close
of business on the last trading day of the month marking the end of the calendar quarter.

Portfolio Assets	Management Fees
First $1 to $1,000,000	1.25%
Next $1,000,001 to $3,000,000	1.00%
Next $3,000,001 to $5,000,000	0.75%
Next $5,000,001 & Over	Negotiable

Either the client or RIA can terminate the client's participation in an ABC Model portfolio
upon thirty days written notice by either party or its legal representative. Notice by the
client of cancellation may be delivered to RIA, Inc. at (address). Notice by RIA will be
sent to the client's address of record. In the event of cancellation, RIA reserves the right
to transfer all ABC Model assets to a "cash" or money market position, unless specific
instructions to the contrary are contained in the cancellation notice. If the client provides
notice of termination in the middle of a quarter, a prorated refund based on the fee
amount paid at the beginning of the quarter will be sent to the client's address of record
within thirty days.

II

Twenty percent of RIA's revenue is generated from the compilation of Financial Plans,
a service available for an hourly charge. The following is a description of the financial-
planning process and the associated charges.

A Financial Plan is an analysis of the individual needs and circumstances of the client. Conducting the process and compilation of a Financial Plan is a mutual decision of the client and RIA. A Financial Plan may or may not be necessary.

If a Financial Plan is mutually deemed appropriate, the Financial Plan will include a detailed information-gathering process with the client regarding objective data such as current investment, income, and financial goals and subjective data such as the client's risk-taking propensity, value system, and sense of priorities. The objective and subjective data can be modular (i.e., only retirement, only estate planning, only college education, etc.) or comprehensive. The written Financial Plan will include an analysis of the client's financial position and will provide recommendations relating to the attainment of the client's Acknowledged Objectives. Recommendations will include the implementation and monitoring of certain investment programs and/or portfolios (ABC Model).

The maximum hourly rate of the process, compilation, and presentation of the Financial Plan (in modular or whole) is $150/hour, charged at fifteen-minute increments. RIA maintains the discretion to charge a lesser hourly rate.

Clients who, at the time of engagement, agree to participate in one of the three ABC Model portfolios described above will receive, if deemed necessary by RIA and the client, a Financial Plan (in whole or modular) at no fee. Reviews, annual or otherwise, will also be at no fee for those clients employing ABC Model portfolios. An annual review of the Financial Plan will be offered to the client.

III

RIA's client base consists of individuals, corporations, trusts, and pension and profit-sharing plans.

IV

The types of investments (products) that RIA uses on behalf of its clients are:

Securities related:
Exchange-listed securities, securities listed over-the-counter, foreign issuers, warrants, corporate debt securities, commercial paper, CDs, municipal securities, variable annuities, mutual fund shares, U.S. government securities, and options

Non-securities related:
Life insurance, long-term care insurance, disability insurance

Not all of these investments are employed on behalf of RIA's clients. These reflect investments in which RIA *might* engage on behalf of the client.

V

RIA employs charting, corporate fundamentals, and technical analysis to perform securities analysis.

VI

RIA utilizes annual corporate reports, corporate press releases, prospectuses, corporate rating services, timing services, research prepared by others, and financial newspapers and magazines as sources of information.

VII

RIA employs the following general investment strategies: long-term purchases, short-term purchases, timing, and trading (securities bought and sold within thirty days).

VIII

RIA investment advisers must have college degrees to provide investment advice.

IX

Billy Goodadvice, RIA Principal, was born August 12, 1958. He received an MBA from Upstate University and an MS and a BS in Liberal Arts from Downstate University. Mr. Goodadvice has been the Principal of RIA since its inception 7/2000. From 12/1987 to 7/2000, Mr. Goodadvice was a partner at SectorVest Group, Inc. in Main Town, Nebraska.

X

Billy Goodadvice is engaged in businesses other than giving investment advice:

LockSoft, LLC (co-principal)—joint venture with two others. A software/Web development firm serving the financial services industry. Average weekly time spent: ten hours (16.7%).

XI

RIA's Principals and Investment Advisers participate in the ABC Model portfolios. To avoid any conflicts of interest during the buying and selling of equities in any of the ABC

Model portfolios, the transactions of the shares of these RIA individuals (that are not "bunched" with RIA clients) will occur in the following manner:

When equities are purchased, all client portfolio equity shares will be purchased before the purchase of those equity shares of RIA individuals.

When equities are sold, all client portfolio equity shares will be sold before the sale of those equity shares of RIA individuals.

XII

RIA's stated minimum to participate in the ABC Model portfolios is $250,000. However, RIA reserves the right to add clients whose investable assets at the time of engagement are below the minimum but will exceed the minimum due to an event (retirement, inheritance, etc.) within the near future.

XIII

RIA's services include various procedures for financial and investment reviews. They are as follows:

ABC Model portfolio annual reviews are offered to RIA clients. It is at the client's discretion to accept or reject an ABC Model portfolio annual review. If the client chooses the annual ABC Model portfolio review, it will include examining diversification shifts, risk tolerance shifts, political and economic conditions, asset performance relative to market, and business cycles. If changes are necessary, they will be implemented after considering tax consequences of such changes. The facts and findings of the Financial Plan (if one was written) or the Suitability Profile will be considered as well. The rebalancing of the client's portfolio is at the mutual discretion of the client and RIA.

RIA's Principal, Billy Goodadvice, performs reviews.

XIV

RIA's services include various reporting methods. They are as follows:

RIA's ABC Model portfolio clients receive monthly account statements from RIA's custodian. In addition, RIA clients receive quarterly performance reports, which include reporting on total portfolio performance and on individual security performance.

XV

Within client accounts, RIA has discretion over which particular securities are bought and sold and the amount of shares of these securities to be bought and sold. With regard to purchase price and number of shares transacted, there are no limitations to RIA's discretionary authority.

XVI

RIA engages other professional entities via a Solicitor's Agreement to refer clients to RIA. Terms of the Solicitor's Agreement provide the other professional entities with compensation for the referrals. RIA's referral agreement is in compliance with the federal regulations as set out in 17 CFR Section 275-206(4)-3, and in each state where state law requires. Each client is given a copy of the referral agreement prior to or at the time of entering into any advisory contract.

Investment Advisory Engagement Agreement

An Agreement between Registered Investment Adviser, LLC, herein referred to as "RIA" and _____ , herein referred to as "The Client."

The Client and RIA agree to the following:

1. The Client acknowledges and accepts that the services provided by RIA include, but are not limited to, management of The Client's investable assets using RIA's proprietary ABC Model for the purpose of seeking rates of return and risk levels consistent with The Client's written and acknowledged objectives. **On behalf of The Client, RIA has discretionary authority to buy or sell equities in the ABC Model portfolio in which The Client's investable assets are placed.**

2. The Investment Advisory service provided by RIA includes:
    a) A written Financial Plan (either modular or comprehensive), if deemed necessary by either The Client or RIA. If a Financial Plan is written, its findings and conclusions will result in Acknowledged Objectives, which will be employed to determine in which ABC Model portfolio The Client's investable assets shall be placed. The Client is obligated to notify RIA in writing at least thirty days in advance of any deviations from any Acknowledged Objectives established by the Financial Plan that The Client wishes to institute.
    If a Financial Plan is not written, a risk/reward analysis and the professional standard Suitability Profile will be employed to determine in which ABC Model portfolio The Client's investable assets shall be placed. The frequency of review of The Client's Suitability Profile is at the discretion of The Client and RIA.
    b) Ongoing monitoring and management of The Client's investable assets using one of RIA's proprietary ABC Model portfolios (detailed under separate, confidential cover).

3. The Client acknowledges that RIA's ABC Model portfolio management style is trademarked and proprietary and that its basis, its methodology, and/or its "Strategic" and/or "Tactical" equity positions in whole cannot be demonstrated to nor shared with nonclients for the purpose of replication.

4. RIA will use "third-party" sources of information, data, and other assistance believed to be reliable and accurate. These sources are integral to evaluating overall circumstances and conditions (economic, political, social, market, management personnel, etc.) and to rendering subsequent recommendations with regard to changes in the ABC Model portfolios.

5. The Client recognizes that ABC Model assets are subject to market and/or other forces that might result in loss of principal and/or earnings. The Client further recognizes and agrees that RIA shall not be liable for any such losses. RIA will exercise prudent care in all actions taken on behalf of The Client's ABC Model assets, yet RIA is neither responsible nor liable for the actions or inactions of any broker, dealer, custodian, or other person or entity (including electronic media) with whom RIA interacts in an effort to serve The Client's interests.

6. RIA opens a custodial account at Trade Inc. Institutional Services for The Client in order to facilitate the execution of all transactions (via the Internet or telephone) and to maintain custody of assets and records. Transaction costs, administrative fees, and custodial charges (if any) are The Client's responsibility. Such charges are provided upon request. Standard practice is to debit Client's account for these charges. Circumstance could necessitate more than one account.

7. For the Investment Advisory service, The Client agrees to pay a "Management Fee." The fee table listed below is annual. The Client's account is charged quarterly, in advance, based on the balance of ABC Model assets on the last business day of the month marking the end of a calendar quarter. If The Client cancels this agreement (as outlined in Clause 9 below) in the middle of a quarter, a prorated fee will be refunded to The Client within thirty days of receipt of the cancellation notice.

Portfolio Assets	Management Fees
First $0 to $1,000,000	1.25%
Next $1,000,001 to $3,000,000	1.00%
Next $3,000,001 to $5,000,000	0.75%
$5,000,001 & Over (Balance of Account)	Negotiable

8. The Client acknowledges that, according to the data from either a Financial Plan or a Suitability Profile, the client's investable assets will be placed in the _____ ABC Model portfolio. _____ (initial)

9. This Agreement is cancelable by either The Client or RIA upon thirty days written notice by either party or its legal representative. Notice by The Client of cancellation may be delivered to RIA at (address). Notice by RIA will be sent to The Client's address of record. In the event of cancellation, RIA reserves the right to transfer all ABC Model assets to a "cash" or money market position, unless specific instructions to the contrary are contained in the cancellation notice. Neither party may assign this Agreement without the written consent of the other party.

10. AGREEMENT TO ARBITRATE CONTROVERSIES: It is agreed that any controversy between or among the undersigned (or any other person[s] or entities who are directly or indirectly a party to this agreement), or any controversy between parties that could relate to RIA's activities as a Registered Investment Adviser (or any other activities pursuant to the terms of this Agreement), shall be submitted to arbitration before the American Arbitration Association, and be handled in accordance with its rules. Arbitration must be commenced when the other party is served with a written demand for arbitration, or by a written notice of intention to arbitrate, therein electing the arbitration tribunal.

11. Investment Advisory services performed by RIA shall be in compliance with the Investment Advisers Act of 1940, rules and regulations thereunder, and applicable U.S. Securities & Exchange Commission laws regulating the services provided by this agreement.

12. The Client acknowledges receipt of RIA's Policies & Procedures and its Form ADV (or its equivalent). _____ (initial)

13. The Client agrees to receive from RIA and TI all performance reports, newsletters, account invoice notices, and other pertinent documents via e-mail (as attachments or in body).
_____ (initial) Such documents will be sent to ALL e-mail addresses below.

Primary e-mail address: _____

Secondary e-mail address: _____

14. The Client warrants that he or she has full power and authority to enter into this Agreement.

THIS AGREEMENT CONTAINS A BINDING PRE-DISPUTE ARBITRATION CLAUSE.
(SEE ITEM 10 ABOVE)

Dated this _____ day of _____ , 20 _____.

Client's Signature: _____

Client's Printed Name: _____

Client's Signature: _____

Client's Printed Name: _____

RIA's Signature: _____

RIA's Printed Name: _____

RIA Sample Operating Agreement Template

Decision-Making Process

♦ Proposal made (by Staff, Associate, or Partner)
♦ Fact-finding w/appropriate Staff, Associate, or Partner
♦ Fact-finding data delivered at the next Partner meeting
♦ Partners debate information, vote on proposal
♦ If accepted, proposal announced and installed
♦ Proposals and their outcomes are in writing, with votes recorded

Decision-Amendment Process

♦ "New Information" (NI) brought to light about a newly accepted proposal
♦ Partners consider the magnitude of and importance of the NI
♦ Partners vote on whether the NI changes the original decision
♦ If the vote is "No," the original decision stands
♦ If the vote is "Yes," the Partners vote to…
  1) vacate the entire proposal, or
  2) change the proposal
♦ If the Partners vote Number 2, changes are debated and incorporated
♦ Partners vote on the reconfigured proposal and announce outcome
♦ Reconfigured proposals and their outcomes are in writing, with votes recorded

Partner Responsibilities

Core: each partner has specific core responsibilities that are compensated by normal revenue flows (either salaries or asset-management fees). At the outset, they are as follows:

Partner 1—Investment Director
Partner 2—New Markets Director
Partner 3—CEO
Partner 4—Principal Adviser
Partner 5—Managing Partner

Non-core: some partners have specific non-core responsibilities for which they may or may not be compensated (either by salary or profit-sharing). At the outset, they are as follows:

Partner 1—None

Partner 2—RIA Compliance Officer

Partner 3—None

Partner 4—None

Partner 5—None

Both Core and Non-core responsibilities can change with majority vote. However, each partner has the right to refuse acceptance of Non-core responsibilities. It is intended that tasks of the Non-core responsibilities be delegated to others (staff or hired specialist) as soon as possible.

Voting: each partner must cast a vote on all issues, even in absentia.

Absentia Voting: partners not able to attend meetings where voting occurs must provide a vote in writing to the Managing Partner prior to the vote itself.

Class A Shares

One Class A share represents $1. Class A shares neither increase nor decrease in value over time. Class A shares have no impact on any and all other means of determining equity ownership in RIA.

Becoming a Founding Partner

Each partner makes an original capital contribution of $50,000 and is issued 50,000 Class A shares in RIA. Each partner agrees to accept the partner responsibilities outlined above.

Becoming a Nonfounding Partner

New partner's current client base and/or business entity is incorporated into or strategically aligned with RIA as negotiated with and voted on by existing partners.

New partner's revenue sharing and equity ownership positions are agreed upon in writing as negotiated and voted on by existing partners.

New partners make a capital contribution to RIA of an amount voted on by the existing partners. New partners are issued Class A shares equal to the amount of capital contribution. New partners agree to accept the partner responsibilities outlined above and those added via addendum.

New partners sign a copy of RIA's Operating Agreement, which includes addendum(s) specifying all pertinent points of new partner's unification with RIA.

Becoming a Nonvoting Partner

If applicable, new nonvoting partner's current client base and/or business entity is incorporated into or strategically aligned with RIA and/or RIA Benefits Group as negotiated with and voted on by existing partners.

New nonvoting partner's revenue sharing and equity ownership positions and/or percentage distributions are agreed upon in writing as negotiated and voted on by existing partners.

New nonvoting partner makes a capital contribution to RIA of an amount voted on by the existing partners. New nonvoting partner is issued Class A shares equal to the amount of capital contribution. New nonvoting partner signs the addendum(s) specifying all pertinent points of new nonvoting partner's unification/relationship with RIA.

Nonvoting partners maintain no voting rights on decisions made by RIA partners.

Becoming an Associate

Associate's current client base is incorporated into RIA as negotiated with and voted on by existing partners. Associate and existing partners negotiate definitive nonpartner, nonstaff responsibilities, and associate signs a document outlining said responsibilities.

Associate signs client ownership agreement stipulating how associate's clients and revenues will be split should the associate leave RIA.

Capital Calls

If necessary, partners will add capital to the partnership if the majority votes that such capital is necessary to continue business operation. For each dollar of capital called, there will be one Class A share distributed.

Class A Share Repurchase

An existing partner's request for a return of part or all of his/her capital contribution requires a majority vote of the existing partners, excluding that of the partner requesting.

However, a request for a return of capital will require a unanimous vote (excluding that of the requesting partner) if such a request would force the existing partners into a capital call.

Decision Making

Partner Group Decisions	OWV*	1P1V**
Significant expense items (> 0.5% annual revenue)	X	
Policy-oriented (i.e., marketing, simplified fee structure, etc.)		X
Personnel matters (organizational restructuring, hiring, firing)		X

* OWV—Ownership-Weighted Vote (based on ownership % as of the last quarter-end)

** 1P1V—One Partner, One Vote

Delegated Decision Making:

Managing partner has spending authorization up to $1,000 without partner approval.

All Other Matters Clause

Decisions regarding all matters not included in this Operating Agreement are subject to a two-thirds vote by the existing partners.

Explanation of Investment (EOI) for Mutual Fund/Variable Annuity

I have reviewed and understand the prospectus and my intended investment. In particular, the following factors have been considered and explained to my satisfaction:

_____ **INVESTMENT GOALS:** I understand that the investment objective(s) is/are (initial all that apply):

_____ Aggressive Growth	_____ Long-Term Income
_____ Moderate Growth	_____ Preservation of Capital
_____ Conservative Growth/Income	_____ Tax Advantage

_____ **VALUE OF SHARES:** I understand the value of my shares in the fund/annuity may go up or down. Depending on the net asset value at the time I redeem my shares, I may receive more or less than I paid for them.

_____ **REDUCED SALES CHARGE:** I am aware I can obtain a reduced sales charge through volume purchases or through agreements to purchase larger amounts over a set period of months.

_____ **CLARIFICATION OF DISTRIBUTIONS:** I am aware that there is no advantage to buying shares in anticipation of a stock dividend or capital gain distribution. The subsequent dividend distribution is actually a par of the offering price and thus becomes a refund of part of my investment.

Choose One:

_____ **COST OF PURCHASE** (Front-End Load Mutual Fund): I understand a sales charge of not more than _____ % of the offering price will be applied against my purchase at the time of purchase.

_____ **COST OF PURCHASE** (Back-End Load Fund or Variable Annuity): I understand a sales charge of not more than _____ % of the offering price will be made. I also understand that a contingent deferred sales charge will apply as outlined in the prospectus, if applicable.

I hereby acknowledge receipt of the prospectus for:

_____

Signed and dated at _____ , _____
this_____ day of _____ , 20_____.

Client's Printed Name: _____
Social Security Number on New Account Form: _____

INVESTOR'S SIGNATURE: _____
(if joint, all must sign)   _____

Registered Representative's Signature: _____
Rep #:_____
Principal's Signature: _____

Mutual Fund/Variable Product Switch Form

Registered Representative Name: _____

Customer Name: _____

Customer Account #: _____

Customer Investment Objective: _____

The following transaction is contemplated:

The **SALE** of _____ ,
which was purchased on _____ for a
commission charged to the customer of $ _____.

The **PURCHASE** of _____
for a commission charged to the customer of $ _____ .

REASON:

_____

_____

_____

_____

_____

_____

_____

_____

Approved by: _____
(Signature of Principal)

Typical Independent Brokerage Firm
Sales Practice Manual Sample Table of Contents

PART ONE—GENERAL

Purpose

Supervisory System

Disciplinary Process

Use of Monikers

Financial Relationships With Clients

Cash & Currency Transactions

Signing Someone Else's Name

Signature Guarantee

Computer Systems and Personal Computers

Internal Documents

Outside Activities

Insider Information

Compliance Department

Surveillance Program

Gifts and Rebates

Relationships With Brokerage Management

Payment of Finders Fees

Receiving Finders Fees

Investment Advisory Activities

Letters of Intent

Training and Education

Payment of Commissions to Registered Reps

Forms & Publications

Bankruptcy

Receipt of Legal Documents

Retention of Outside Attorneys

Contact With Industry Regulators

Legal Testimony

Criminal Matters

Regulatory Matters

PART TWO—REGISTRATION & LICENSING

Form U-4

Securities Registration of Registered Reps

Options Registration

Municipal 529 Principal Registration

Investment Advisory Agent Registration

Insurance Registration

Commission Sharing

Activities of Unregistered Personnel

Termination of Registration

Form U-5

PART THREE—BRANCHES & SATELLITES

Definition

Registration

Brokerage Identification

Branch Office Files

Incoming Mail (Including Faxes & E-mails)

Outgoing Mail (Including Faxes & E-mails)

Fingerprinting

Receiving Checks and Securities

Banking Methods

Branch Audits and Inspections

PART FOUR—NEW ACCOUNTS

Know Your Clients

Opening Brokerage Accounts

Opening Nonbrokerage Accounts

Suitability

Direct Deposit

Account Transfers

Block Transfers of Mutual Funds or Annuities

Guaranteed Accounts

Trust Accounts

UGMA/UTMA Accounts

PART SEVEN—MUTUAL FUND TRANSACTIONS

Suitability

Purchases

Statements

Redemptions

Order Entry

Disclosure

Breakpoints

Switches

No-Loads

Dealer-Use-Only Material

Change of Broker/Dealer

PART EIGHT—VARIABLE PRODUCTS

Registration and Licensing

Suitability

Replacement

Purchasing a Variable Product

Contract Delivery

PART NINE—RECORDKEEPING REQUIREMENTS

Client Holding Records

Client Security File

Recordkeeping

Record Retention

Disbursements From a Client's Account

Change of Client Status
Updating Client Personal and Financial Information

Delivery of Securities

Delivery of Checks to Clients

Transfer of Funds or Securities From a Custodial Account

Account Evaluations/Performance Reports

Brokerage Account Fees

Dividend Reinvestment Program (DRIP)

PART TEN—PLACING ORDERS

PART ELEVEN—HANDLING CLIENT COMPLAINTS

Internet Resources

THE WEBSITE OF the Securities and Exchange Commission (SEC) is a good place to start when looking for the answer to any securities questions, other than extraordinary ones: **www.sec.gov.**

This address quickly burrows down to the SEC's pages that are devoted primarily to Registered Investment Advisers: **www.sec.gov/divisions/investment.shtml.**

Also at the SEC address is information for broker/dealers: **www.sec.gov/divisions/marketreg.shtml.**

The NASD website (**www.nasd.com**) deals only with issues of the Registered Representative (a.k.a. its members). To get to the NASD rules, go to that page and click on the Rules & Regulations tab on the top. The links on the left of this page will take you to specific areas of concern.

At the website **http://www.law.uc.edu/CCL/xyz/sldtoc.html**, you can find the text of the Securities Act of 1934 and all its subsequently passed rules and regulations, as well as the Investment Advisers Act of 1940 and all its subsequent rules and regulations.

The NASD registration management site is **https://www.webiard.com.** This site is password/username protected, which means that you must first become either a broker-dealer or an RIA to engage its content. This is where those entities go to manage their affairs with either the NASD or the SEC. The SEC has turned over the maintenance of the site to the NASD, even for RIAs.

For state security regulator contacts, go to **www.nasaa.org**. On the left navigation bar, click on Contact Your Regulator. This will take you to a map of the United States and Canada. Click on the state of interest for information.

Ameritas Direct is a low-load life insurance provider: **www.ameritas direct.com**.

At **www.dearborn.com**, you can access all general securities licensing educational (testing) material. Click on Securities Licensing on the left navigation bar. Follow the instructions on this page; it's quite easy to navigate.

For an exhaustive discussion about broad regulatory issues for RIAs, go to this SEC page: **www.sec.gov/divisions/investment/roundtable/ iadvrndt.htm**.

There are numerous securities compliance consultants on the market. These are but two of them: **www.ncsonline.com** and **www .nrs-inc.com**.

If you're saddled with procuring your own Errors & Omissions insurance, this might be a good place to start: **www.prosurancegroup .com/**.

Do you want securities forms (ADV, U-4, U-5, etc.)? Go here to find any and all: **www.nasaa.org**. Pass your mouse over the Industry & Regulatory Resources tab. Then choose Uniform Forms.

If you're interested (and you should be) in abiding by e-mail compliance regulations, no matter what size your firm, you should check out this software: **http://www.compliancecompany.com/**.

And finally, the author's contact info (in case you pitched the paper jacket to this book): **tgrady@trinitywealth.com**. Mr. Grady conducts workshops and seminars, and consults on the topics of this book.

Index

active ownership/partnership, of
RIA, 73–83, 86–87, 157–173
ADV. *See under* Securities and
Exchange Commission
alliances, with RIAs, 57–83, 85–86,
125–179. *See also* revenue-
sharing rate
active ownership/partnership,
73–83, 86–87, 157–173
in general, 57–58, 125–129
investment advisor, 47, 64–67, 72,
86, 139–147
passive ownership/partnership,
67–72, 86, 147–157, 209
solicitor's agreement, 59–64, 72,
85–86, 129–139, 208
alliances, with RRs, 43–44, 101–
124. *See also* compensation
consulting services, 41, 121–124
with employed RRs, 103–110
in general, 101–103
with independent RRs, 110–117
leasing space to independent RRs,
11, 40–41, 117–121
"all-talk" alliance, reasons for failure
of, 1–4
annuities, variable
RIA fees and, 54–55, 56–57
RR commissions and, 36–38
sample EOI for, 235–236
applications, for new brokerage or

mutual fund account
RIA compliance and, 97
RR compliance and, 90
approval method, in RIA alliance, 58
active ownership/partnership, 168
investment advisor, 66, 142
passive ownership/partnership,
71, 152
solicitor's agreement, 63, 131
asset management programs, of
RIAs, 50–54
audits
of RIAs, 9, 100
of RRs, 8–9, 30, 95–96
authority to advise, of RRs, 39
automated customer account transfer
(ACAT)
RIA compliance and, 98
RR compliance and, 92
automatic clearing house (ACH)
RIA compliance and, 98
RR compliance and, 92
autonomous associated RIA, 46–49,
83–84, 125
autonomous unassociated RIA, 48–
49, 84, 125

Bernstein, Phyllis, quoted, 21
"booked referral" ownership, in RIA
alliance, 57
investment advisor, 65

245

passive ownership/partnership, 68
solicitor's agreement, 62
breakpoints, of mutual fund shares,
34, 91
brokerage affiliation disclosure, of
RRs, 19, 20
brokerage-based RIA, 46–49, 83–
84, 125
brokerage firms, types of, 27
buyout provision, in RIA alliance, 58
active ownership/partnership, 168
investment advisor, 66, 143
passive ownership/partnership,
71, 152–153
solicitor's agreement, 63, 133

capital contribution, in RIA alliance,
57
active ownership/partnership, 158
investment advisor, 65, 140
passive ownership/partnership, 69,
148–149
solicitor's agreement, 62, 129
Carter, Sarah, 201
case studies
Fredrick Withers, CPA, 195–198
Horizon Financial Advisors, LLC,
199–205
clarification of distributions, in RR's
EOI, 91
client's investment goals, in RR's
EOI, 91
client advocacy
in RIA alliance, 137–138, 146,
155–156, 171
in RR alliance, 108–109, 115,
120, 123
client securities-related communications
RIA compliance, 98–99
RR compliance, 93–94
commissions, for RRs, 28

administration of, 31–32
ERR alliance, 104–105, 107, 109
IRR alliance, 110–111, 113,
115–116, 117, 118, 120, 121,
123–124
non-disclosure of, 18–19
by product, 32–39
communications. *See* client securities-
related communications
compensation, for RIA alliances,
133–134, 136, 143–144, 153,
169. *See also* fees and services
compliance
for RIA, 96–100
for RIA alliance, 134, 144, 153,
169
for RR, 89–96
for RR alliance, 105, 111–112,
117–118, 121
consulting services, of RRs, 11, 41,
121–124
contingent deferred sales charge
(CDSC)
on Class B mutual fund shares, 35
on variable annuities, 37–38
continuing education. *See* training
and education
cost of purchase, in RR's EOI, 91–92

Darrah, John R., 185, 189, 191, 193
Diliberto, Roy T., quoted, 22
disclosure. *See* prospectus; SEC Form
ADV
duals, 25

e-mail, compliance and, 94
employed registered representative
(ERR), 17, 32, 101. *See also*
registered representative
contrasted to independent registered representative, 27–31, 43
CPA as registered representative

About Bloomberg

Bloomberg L.P., founded in 1981, is a global information services, news, and media company. Headquartered in New York, the company has sales and news operations worldwide.

Bloomberg, serving customers on six continents, holds a unique position within the financial services industry by providing an unparalleled range of features in a single package known as the BLOOMBERG PROFESSIONAL® service. By addressing the demand for investment performance and efficiency through an exceptional combination of information, analytic, electronic trading, and Straight Through Processing tools, Bloomberg has built a worldwide customer base of corporations, issuers, financial intermediaries, and institutional investors.

BLOOMBERG NEWS®, founded in 1990, provides stories and columns on business, general news, politics, and sports to leading newspapers and magazines throughout the world. BLOOMBERG TELEVISION®, a 24-hour business and financial news network, is produced and distributed globally in seven languages. BLOOMBERG RADIO℠ is an international radio network anchored by flagship station BLOOMBERG® 1130 (WBBR-AM) in New York.

In addition to the BLOOMBERG PRESS® line of books, Bloomberg publishes *BLOOMBERG MARKETS*® magazine. To learn more about Bloomberg, call a sales representative at:

London: +44-20-7330-7500
New York: +1-212-318-2000
Tokyo: +81-3-3201-8900

FOR IN-DEPTH MARKET INFORMATION and news, visit the Bloomberg website at **www.bloomberg.com**, which draws from the news and power of the BLOOMBERG PROFESSIONAL® service and Bloomberg's host of media products to provide high-quality news and information in multiple languages on stocks, bonds, currencies, and commodities.

About the Author

Thomas Grady is one of five partners and the chief compliance officer at Trinity Wealth Group in St. Louis, Missouri. Trinity Wealth Group comprises three divisions: Life Wealth Management, Investment Management, and Business Succession/Retirement. Trinity was ranked among the top twenty-eight U.S. investment advisory firms in 2004 by Schwab Institutional in its comprehensive *Best Managed Firms* survey. (An affiliate, Trinity Wealth Securities, is the firm's broker/dealer.) Mr. Grady's firm engages CPAs, banks, and other related entities and individuals in the revenue-sharing strategic alliances described in this book. He oversees this part of his firm's business and is responsible for the regulatory matters involved.

Mr. Grady has written articles for *Financial Planning* and *Bloomberg Wealth Manager* magazines, and he conducts seminars and workshops and consults on the topics covered in his book. He can be reached at tgrady@trinitywealth.com.

Mr. Grady was born and raised in St. Louis. He holds a BS and an MS in liberal arts, and an MBA. He served proudly in the U.S. Air Force from 1970 through 1974.